SEASONS

IN THE

DESERT

a naturalist's notebook

BY

susan j. tweit

ILLUSTRATIONS BY

kirk caldwell

CHRONICLE BOOKS
SAN FRANCISCO

Several of the essays are modified from
pieces that originally appeared in maga-
zines, as follows: "Tumbleweed" in NEW
MEXICO magazine, November 1993
(Tumbling Tumbleweeds); "Giant Desert
Centipede" in HARROWSMITH COUNTRY
LIFE, May/June 1993 (Creepy Crawly);
"Fairy Shrimp" in HARROWSMITH COUNTRY
LIFE, May/June 1992 (Puddle Puzzle);
"Coyote" in CRICKET, THE MAGAZINE
FOR KIDS, June 1996 (Coyotes Come to
Town) and HARROWSMITH COUNTRY LIFE,
March/April 1991 (Song Dogs in the
Backyard); and "Creosote Bush" in NEW
MEXICO magazine, April 1992. "Night-
blooming Cereus" is modified from "Coming
to the Chihuahuan Desert" in BARREN,
WILD, AND WORTHLESS: LIVING IN THE
CHIHUAHUAN DESERT (University of New
Mexico Press, 1995).

Quote on page 8 in Introduction is ex-
cerpted from "Why Albuquerque?" © 1942
by Ernie Pyle. Reprinted with permission of
NEW MEXICO MAGAZINE. Quote on page 14
in "Night-blooming Cereus" is excerpted
from DESERT LEGENDS: RE-STORYING THE
SONORAN BORDERLANDS by Gary Paul
Nabhan, pages 41–42, © 1995 Gary Paul
Nabhan. Reprinted by permission of Henry
Holt & Co., Inc. Quote on page 33 in
"Tumbleweed" is excerpted from "Tumblin'
Tumbleweeds" by Bob Nolan. All rights
reserved. Reprint permission granted
by Music of the West c/o The Songwriters
Guild of America. Quote on page 59
in "Couch's Spadefoot Toad" is excerpted
from THE BEAN TREES by Barbara King-
solver, pages 163–164, © 1988 Barbara
Kingsolver. Reprinted by permission of
HarperCollins Publishers, Inc. Quote on
page 64 in "Ocotillo" is excerpted from
letter by Dr. William A. Cannon in the
MacDougal Collection, Arizona Historical

Society. Reprinted with permission of
Library/Archives Department, Arizona
Historical Society. Quote on page 69 in
"Costa's Hummingbird" is excerpted from
THE TATTOOED LADY IN THE GARDEN,
© 1989 by Wesleyan University Press.
Reprinted with permission of University
Press of New England. Quote on page 164
in "Chihuahuan Raven" is excerpted from
DESERT NOTES: REFLECTIONS IN THE EYE OF
A RAVEN, © 1976 Barry Holston Lopez.
Reprinted by permission of Sterling Lord
Literistic.

Printed in Hong Kong.

Library of Congress Cataloging-in-
Publication Data:
Tweit, Susan J.
    Seasons in the desert: a naturalist's
notebook/Susan J. Tweit: illustrations by
Kirk Caldwell.
        p. cm.
    Includes bibliographical references.
ISBN 0-8118-1685-0 (hc)
1. Desert animals. 2. Desert plants. 3.
Seasons. I. Title.
QH88.T84 1998
578.754—dc21   97-11384
                                                CIP

Book and jacket design: Carole Goodman
Composition: Neal Elkin/On Line Type
Cover illustration: Costa's Hummingbird by
Kirk Caldwell

Distributed in Canada by Raincoast Books
8680 Cambie Street
Vancouver, B.C. V6P 6M9

10 9 8 7 6 5 4 3 2 1

Chronicle Books
85 Second Street
San Francisco, CA 94105

Web Site: www.chronbooks.com

For Jennie, who loves the desert —
may this bring sunshine to even the
foggiest of your days!

a c k n o w l e d g m e n t s

The idea for this book came from WILD LIVES, my long-running series of nature spots on southern New Mexico–west Texas public radio. Special thanks to Tom Huizenga, Ann Palormo, Kathy DeAguero, and to David Brower, for their parts in bringing WILD LIVES to the air. *Y gracias, tambien*, to KRWG radio, its sponsors, and to the enthusiastic listeners who comment on the show.

Many people answered my questions and helped me find sources of information. Thanks to the reference librarians at New Mexico State University, including Laural Adams, Tim McKimmie, and Roger Steeb, and to Lilia Fernandez at the library of University of Texas–El Paso. *Gracias tambien a* Dave Anderson, botanist, White Sands Missile Range; Patricia C. Arrowood, ornithologist, New Mexico State University; Jayne Belnap, biologist, Canyonlands National Park; Donna Howell, bat biologist; Gary Paul Nabhan, director of science, Arizona–Sonora Desert Museum; Dave Richman, entomologist, New Mexico State University; Linda Sweanor and Ken Logan, mountain lion biologists; Mara Weisenberger, biologist, San Andres National Wildlife Refuge; and Caroline Wilson, Arizona–Sonora Desert Museum.

Muchas gracias a Jennifer McDonald, my agent—this book is for you, and Sarah. And to Karen Silver, who loved the book from the beginning—I feel privileged to work with you. *Gracias, tambien*, to Kirk Caldwell, for his illustrator's eye. To my three editors—it was a rare pleasure to read your dialog on the pages. Thanks especially to copyeditor Anne Hayes for her lucid and illuminating work. Designer Carole Goodman made the book beautiful and inviting, for which I thank her. And *muchas gracias, tambien*, to the publicists, marketing people, the sales reps, and the rest of the staff at Chronicle Books—without you, my book wouldn't reach its audience. Thanks also to the photocopy staff at Insta-Copy Printing for meticulous and patient color copy work.

I am blessed by a network of friends whose lives enrich mine. I thank you all for your strength and the lessons you have taught me. *Gracias especialmente* to Denise Chávez, Elena Linthicum, Pam Porter, and Patricia Wendel. And to Alison Hawthorne Deming, who generously encouraged me to send my work to Jennie McDonald—thank you for that faith! Thanks also to Lisa Brown, Kristen Casteel, Judy Darnall, Sandra Lynn, Lisa Dale Norton, Ann Palormo, Linda Peterson, Mary Ransome, Ursula Shepherd, Terry Tempest Williams, and to the Las Cruces Friends Meeting. And to my companions on various desert explorations: Richard and Molly Cabe, Barbara and Harold Harrison, J. David Love, Blanche Sobottke, and Carol Warden—no landscape is so magical as one shared. And to *mi perrita*, Perdida, whose heart's desire is to go along, no matter the destination. Special thanks, as well, to the late Elizabeth Fleming McFarland, for the generous gift of books from her own library, and the inspiration from her life and writing.

I owe a great deal to my family. Thanks with many hugs to my parents, Joan and Bob Tweit, who not only nurtured my love for the desert, but who cheerfully looked up obscure facts and sources of information, and whose sharp editorial eyes I rely on. Thanks to all the rest of my family, Tweit, Winter, Cabe, and Hitz, for cheering me on—your words of support mean more than you know. *Y gracias con besitos a mi esposo y mi'ija,* Richard and Molly Cabe, who have walked with me, listened to my ideas, and whose love is the greatest gift of all.

Any errors, misinterpretations, or omissions are, of course, entirely my own responsibility.

table of contents

introduction

We like it because the sky is so bright and you can see so much of it. And because out here you actually see the clouds and the stars and the storms, instead of just reading about them in the newspapers. They become a genuine part of your daily life, and half the entire horizon is yours in one glance for the looking, and the distance sort of gets into your soul and makes you feel that you too are big inside.
—Ernie Pyle, "Why Albuquerque?" THE SPELL OF NEW MEXICO

What is a desert? Dictionary definitions speak of barrenness and desolation. Scientific definitions hinge on life. Deserts are defined by such extremes. They are characterized by extreme aridity, by low and irregularly distributed annual precipitation in particular—months and months of no rain, then a summer thunderstorm dumps three inches in an hour. Deserts are also characterized by extremes of temperature, both heat and cold. Days get hot, especially during summer when temperatures routinely rise above the hundred mark. But with dry air and very little insulating cloud cover, deserts lose heat quickly at night—swings of 40 degrees from day to night are normal. (Imagine going from winter to summer and back again every twenty-four hours!) Added to the unreliable moisture and widely fluctuating daily temperatures are high solar radiation, dry air, and regular, persistent wind. Together, these add up to extreme evaporative potential: a climate that can suck up far more moisture than it ever delivers.

The "desert" of the title is the North American desert, stretching from southeastern Oregon and southern Idaho south into central México. This broad expanse is arid because it lies in the rain shadow of the Sierra Nevada and the Cascade Range, mountain masses large enough to wring much of the life-giving moisture from Pacific Ocean storms before they reach the interior of the continent. The North American desert is actually made up of four distinct parts: the Great Basin, Mojave, Sonoran, and the Chihuahuan Deserts. Each is characterized by a dominant plant or plants, a particular temperature regime and season of precipitation, and a distinct rhythm to the landscape.

The Great Basin, the northernmost and highest desert—it lies above 4,000 feet elevation—covers most of Nevada and stretches into southeastern Oregon, southern Idaho, and western Utah. Big sagebrush is its characteristic plant, although salt-tolerant plants like saltbush replace sagebrush on extensive alkali flats. This is a "cold" desert. Daytime highs in summer may top 100 degrees, but winter lows routinely drop into the minus numbers. Most of its annual precipitation—over 60 percent—comes in winter from Pacific Ocean storms, and falls as snow. The cadence of this landscape is a regular alternation of highs and lows: flat, arid basin, high, finlike mountain range; basin, range; basin, range ... and so on, for mile after mile.

The Mojave, the desert of Joshua trees, borders the Great Basin Desert on the south. This sparse desert covers the southern tip of Nevada, much of southeastern California, and the extreme northeastern edge of Arizona. It is North America's smallest and driest desert—some parts of the Mojave have gone two years without precipitation! It is also the most westerly desert and thus, like the Great Basin, receives essentially all of its moisture from storms rolling east off the Pacific Ocean in winter. But because the Mojave is farther south and lower than the Great Basin, its precipitation comes as rain. This is a "hot" desert. The highest temperature on the North American continent—134 degrees—was recorded here, at Death Valley, the lowest point on the continent. The Mojave rolls in a gentle, swelling rhythm: its in-draining basins sliding gently up at the edges to meet the rocky slopes of low mountain ranges.

The Sonoran, the hottest and wettest of the four deserts, runs from the south edge of the Mojave in extreme southeastern California east through southern Arizona to touch the Chihuahuan Desert, then south through Baja California and Sonora, México. Saguaro and other tree-sized cacti characterize this nearly tropical desert. Its combination of generally low elevations (sea level up to 3,400 feet) and southerly location turn up the heat year-round, except in the scattered mountain ranges. The Sonoran boasts winter *and* summer rainy seasons, making it the most verdant of the North American deserts. The landscape is an abrupt contrast between extremes: a sea of hot, low-elevation desert broken by the cool heights of islandlike mountain ranges.

The Chihuahuan, North America's largest desert, touches the Sonoran Desert at its western extent in southeastern Arizona and sprawls farther east than any other North American desert, reaching across west Texas to Big Bend. This huge desert runs nearly a thousand miles north to south, from central New Mexico to San Luis Potosí, México. Despite high average elevations (above 3,500 feet), the Chihuahuan is a "hot" desert because it lies so far south. Unlike the other three deserts, this desert receives very little winter moisture: 60 to 80 percent of its annual precipitation comes in summer, from storms that originate on the Gulf of Mexico. Agaves, huge relatives of lilies, characterize this desert. The cadence of the Chihuahuan is a nearly even tone: wide, flat-floored basins stretch almost from horizon to horizon, interrupted now and again by narrow, linear mountain ranges.

This book is a naturalist's family album. It profiles forty desert plants and animals, a small sample of the incredible diversity of the North American deserts. I think of these desert characters as my relatives, in the sense that all life is kin; these particular kin are lives I know very well. I've selected an assortment as idiosyncratic as any family: the lives profiled here may represent some important adaptation to desert life, or a significant relationship; they may be characteristic of a particular desert, or they may be included simply because I like them.

The profiles are grouped by season, depending on what time of the year each plant or creature is most prominent or on some seasonal event in the story of their lives. Each opens with the name of the plant or animal in English, Spanish (an important language throughout most of the desert region), and its scientific name, and then a quote relating to the profile. Following the quote is a paragraph giving the facts about the creature or plant's life: what its names mean, how big it is, what color, where it lives, and other details. Then comes the "family story," a personal essay about that particular desert life and how I know it. At the back of the book is a short glossary of habitats, and "Recommended Reading and Places to Visit," a section giving tips on where to read more about that particular plant or creature and a suggestion on where or how to see it.

I hope that you will read this book as you would a family album, with affection, interest, and a renewed sense of the kinship we have with all life. May the stories of these wild relatives bring the desert home to you.

SPRING

Spring does not creep across the desert on little cat's feet; nor does it come in with frolicking lambs and sweet breezes. Spring—the season beginning with the spring equinox and ending with the summer solstice—can bring an explosion of vibrant and colorful life; it can be a succession of frigid snowstorms; it can blow in dry and hot on gritty winds. How spring comes to the various deserts depends on the latitude and rainfall pattern of each, and on the weather of any given year.

The North American deserts are watered by two major storm tracks: the cold, soggy storms that roar east across the continent in winter from the Pacific Ocean, and the warm, wet fronts that circle north and west in summer from the Gulf of Mexico and the Gulf of California. Whether spring is relatively green or not in the various deserts depends on which storm track they are under. The three deserts that lie farthest west—the Great Basin, Mojave, and Sonoran—are the closest to the Pacific Ocean and thus reliably receive winter moisture. Their springs are relatively wet. The southernmost of these three deserts—the Mojave and Sonoran—explode with life in wet springs, the formerly bare soil covered by a carpet of annual plants. Spring in the Chihuahuan Desert, by contrast, is a dry time, since moisture from the Pacific rarely reaches this easternmost desert.

Look for wildflower displays as early as late February, first in the Mojave at places like Death Valley National Park, and in the lowest elevations of the Sonoran Desert. Annual wildflowers bloom somewhere in these two deserts nearly every year, sometime between

February and May, germinating, growing, flowering, and setting seed in the space of a few weeks. Every seven years or so, the rains are just right for annual seed germination and the entire landscape blossoms. For a short time, the deserts seem like lush, verdant places. Then the soils dry out and these ephemeral plants shatter and disappear, leaving their seeds to wait for another good year. Scientists still do not understand exactly what combination of rainfall and temperature is necessary to initiate these spectacular displays.

Despite wet springs from melting snow, the Great Basin Desert doesn't boast bounteous spring wildflower displays: its soils are too cold. It does turn green in spring, however, as the grasses begin to grow. The temporary abundance of water begins to pool in shallow lakes formed in the low spots of in-draining basins. An explosion of lives colonizes the ephemeral waters of such playa lakes, from resident fairy shrimp to migrating American avocets. The Chihuahuan Desert, by contrast, is warm enough for wildflower germination, but too dry: it lies too far east to receive much moisture from the winter storms. Spring in the Chihuahuan Desert is wind season—as the land dries out and heats up, westerly winds sweep across it, kicking up tumbleweeds and clouds of soil. Look for spectacular mirages in the Chihuahuan Desert in spring. Caused by sharp discontinuities in air temperature which reflect light waves like mirrors, mirages develop best when the ground is dry and can heat up, but when the air remains cool.

Spring is migration season in the deserts. Look for hummingbirds feeding at ocotillo blossoms and other red, tubular flowers. Scan the ephemeral lakes in desert basins formed by melting snow and winter rains for migrating shorebirds, ducks, pelicans, and sandhill cranes. The glittering waters of these temporary aquatic environments act like beacons to migrants passing high above the desert's thirsty landscapes, broadcasting the promise of a hospitable respite from their long journeys.

Night-blooming Cereus

Reina-de-la-noche
Peniocereus greggii

> ... I stumbled into a cereus population at dusk. At first, from a distance, I thought someone had left some flashlights on, dropped out among the desert scrub. As I walked closer to some ironwoods and creosote, the flashlights turned to flowers. I couldn't believe my tired eyes.... They were gorgeous! The ugly ducklings had metamorphosed into swans!
>
> —Gary Paul Nabhan, DESERT LEGENDS: RE-STORYING THE SONORAN BORDERLANDS

NAME: Night-blooming cereus refers to the night-opening, star-like flowers. *Reina-de-la-noche*, the plant's Spanish name, means "queen of the night," a reference to the glorious blossoms as well. *Cereus* means "star" in Latin; *greggii* commemorates Josiah Gregg, a frontier trader and author who traveled widely in northern México and the Southwest in the 1840s.

SIZE: Stems reach 6½ feet long but are only about a half-inch in diameter; flowers to five inches across

COLOR: Stems lead-colored, flowers silky white, fruits dull red

RANGE: The Sonoran and Chihuahuan Deserts of northern México and southern Arizona, southern New Mexico, and southwest Texas

HABITAT: Gravely or silty soils in washes and flats; grows within canopy of desert shrubs

Deserts are deceptive landscapes. For much of the year, they look bleak, barren, dead. But add water—whether from melting snow or warm rain—and these forbidding landscapes awaken, revealing life in an exuberant riot of color and form. The bare soil sprouts a carpet of wildflowers in vivid hues. Shrubs that appeared dead suddenly sprout new green leaves. For a short time—until the water evaporates—the landscape is flush with life.

One of the masters of this kind of deception is a cactus that grows in the harshest parts of the Sonoran and Chihuahuan Deserts. Most people never notice this plant: the cactus's slender, deeply ribbed stems grow hidden within the canopies of shrubs or small trees like creosote bush and mesquite. (The stems' shape and color, in fact, mimic those of their host plant.) When you do spot this cactus, what you see is not impressive: sprawling, gray, sticklike stems studded with long spines. The unprepossessing appearance belies the plant's beautiful Spanish name, *reina-de-la-noche*, "queen of the night."

Each spring, however, the plant undergoes a magical transformation from ugly duckling to swan. The upper portions of the scrawny stems sprout buds, which swell, and swell, and swell. One night in summer, the buds burst open into enormous, silky white flowers up to five inches across and shaped like many-petaled stars. The glorious blossoms broadcast a musky, intensely sweet fragrance on the night air, as seductive as any fine perfume.

The fragrance is a necessary advertisement, a come-hither call to lure partners to fertilize the blossoms. Timing is everything, since each flower only lasts one night and flowers may open on as few as four nights in a given summer, depending on the occurrence and intensity of the summer rains. The persistent scent lures night-flying nectar-drinkers, including sphinx moths, to the plants to drink the food buried deep in each flower's base. As they hover and sip, these nighttime visitors brush against the flower's sex organs. Emerging coated with a dusting of lemon-yellow pollen grains, the moths fly on to the next flower and thus pollinate it as they slurp its sweet nectar.

The partnership between hovering moths and night-blooming cereus is a necessary one, says botanist Gary Paul Nabhan. The cactus's flowers are self-incompatible —that is, they require pollen from another night-blooming cereus plant to reproduce—and the plants grow far apart, in densities as low as five to ten per acre, so they depend on a rambling partner like a sphinx moth to carry pollen from plant to distant plant. Sphinx moths benefit as well: they need the high sugar content of flower nectar to fuel their hovering flight. *Reina-de-la-noche* is among the few night-blooming species that the hovering moths depend on.

Sphinx moths, named for the larvae's habit of raising one end of its body in a threatening, sphinxlike posture, are unusual creatures themselves. With stout, furry bodies, long, narrow wings, and wingspans from two to six inches, these improbable beings look like a cross between bats and hummingbirds. To see a heavy-bodied sphinx moth hover delicately above a flower is to believe in the miracle of flight. Indeed, the study of sphinx moths' hovering revolutionized our understanding of insects. Scientists once believed that insects were poikilotherms, cold-blooded beings that cannot regulate their body temperature internally, as "advanced" animals can. But a hovering sphinx moth generates heat, in fact enough heat to stew its own body. If they cannot regulate their own body temperature internally, how do sphinx moths keep cool? At first, scientists assumed that sphinx moths were restricted to flying only when air temperatures were cool enough to keep their bodies from cooking. A neat explanation, but it doesn't fit: their massive flight muscles cannot operate at cool temperatures.

Intrigued by the mystery, entomologist Bernd Heinrich attached tiny temperature probes to flying sphinx moths and found that they can indeed regulate their own body temperatures internally. When conditions are too cool, Heinrich discovered, sphinx moths shiver to warm themselves up by firing the synapses of their flight muscles synchronously, generating a great deal of heat but no flight. Once airborne, however, that heat becomes a liability. To keep from overheating, Heinrich found, sphinx moths circulate hot blood through their abdomen, using its large surface area as an air-cooled radiator.

Reina-de-la-noche's lavish blossoms each last only one night, and then wilt. Their ephemeral beauty is legendary. That such splendor should suddenly spring from a scrawny plant seems impossible, something born of magic. Indeed, it springs from an extraordinary ability to harvest desert resources—the energy from sunlight, nutrients from the soil, and water from infrequent desert rainstorms. This cactus hoards its hard-won stores underground in a swollen, several-foot-long tap root, which can weigh up to a hundred pounds and which resembles the parsnip from hell. Once a year, the cactus draws on its provisions to produce the glorious blossoms. *Reina-de-la-noche* exemplifies for me the magic of deserts: a harsh, seemingly ugly and lifeless exterior capable of suddenly producing extravagant beauty.

One June when my husband Richard, my daughter Molly, and I were visiting my parents, my mother woke us in the night, flashlight in hand. "Come see!" she whispered. We sleepily slipped on shoes and trailed her into the desert behind their house. Under a scraggly shrub, her flashlight illuminated half a dozen of the biggest, most brilliant white flowers we'd ever seen. She switched off the light, and the many-petaled blossoms glowed in the sudden darkness. "Oh," breathed Molly, her young voice rapt with wonder, "fallen stars!"

Sadly, the queen of the night is disappearing. Plant thieves search out the scrawny plants, dig them up, and sell them. Domestic livestock searching for food in overgrazed desert areas trample the cactus's fragile stems. And in some places, Gary Paul Nabhan reports, their partners in pollination have disappeared, wiped out by agricultural pesticides. This last may be the most serious threat—because it is so final. When the relationships that make up ecosystems are severed, the fabric of the ecosystem itself is imperiled. Eventually, the fabric may grow so weak that it can no longer support life— including our own.

The story of *reina-de-la-noche* is truly a metaphor for the deserts. The fate of these beautiful and deceptive cacti, like the fate of the ecosystems that nurture them, lies in our hands. When we lose night-blooming cereus, we lose not only the other species dependent on them, but we lose the alchemy of their blossoming as well. Will we discover the value of desert ecosystems in time to save their tough and enduring magic? A world without the sudden radiance of night-blooming cereus and the improbable hovering of sphinx moths would be an impoverished world, indeed.

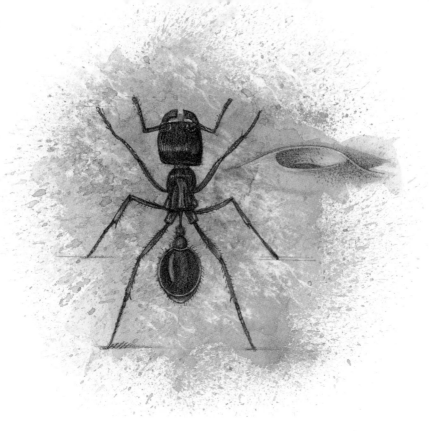

ROUGH HARVESTER ANT

Hormiga
Pogonomyrmex rugosus

> *If all of humanity were to disappear, the remainder of life would spring back and flourish.... If all the ants somehow disappeared, the effect would be exactly the opposite, and catastrophic.*
> —Bert Hölldobler and Edward O. Wilson, JOURNEY TO THE ANTS

NAME: Harvester ants are named for their feeding activity: they forage for seeds. *Hormiga* means "ant" in Spanish. *Pogonomyrmex* means "bearded ant" in Greek, a reference to the hairs that cover the bodies of these big ants; *rugosus*, or "wrinkled" in Latin, apparently refers to the rough look caused by the coarse hairs.

SIZE: Up to one-half inch long, depending on the caste, with a large, helmetlike head and massive jaws

COLOR: Black head and rust red abdomen

RANGE: The most conspicuous ant in the deserts, found throughout the southwestern United States and northern México

HABITAT: Areas of sandy or silty soil from basin floors up to the woodlands of the lower mountains

NOTES: Nest entrances are surrounded by a mound up to two feet across. Beyond that, they may graze bare an area many feet in diameter.

On a July evening in 1975, entomologist Bert Hölldobler stumbled on an extraordinary find: a harvester ant mating ground. It was, as he describes in *Journey to the Ants,* an area in the open desert the size of a tennis court, where the ground was "roiling" with big, winged ants. Hölldobler watched, fascinated, as thousands of harvester ant queens flew in, lit on the ground, and were rushed by eager males. Once successfully inseminated, a queen rubbed two body segments together, making a squeaking noise. At that signal, her suitors dropped off and rushed away to pursue another female. The mated queen flew away; the males stayed on for more trysts.

The discovery of this harvester ant lekking ground surprised Hölldobler and other myrmecologists (scientists who study ants). Vertebrate animals such as sage grouse and pronghorn antelope were known to gather at a lek, a sort of wild Lover's Lane, to court and mate, but not ants. Further, Hölldobler found, the harvester ants returned to the exact same spot to mate July after July. Yet, each year's eager suitors were a brand-new generation—how did they know to fly to that spot in the desert? What signals and genetic memories trigger such gatherings? We do not know.

Harvester ants are the largest and most conspicuous ants in the deserts. Like all ants, they are social insects, members of highly organized colonies numbering from a few dozen to millions of individuals. A mated queen founds a colony by first nibbling off her now-useless wings, and then scratching out a small chamber in the soil and laying a batch of eggs. (Her mate and the other males of her generation die soon after the mating flights.) She survives without eating as this first generation grows by metabolizing her flight muscles and the fat in her own body. After the offspring mature, however, they care for her, leaving the queen with literally nothing to do but lie around and reproduce. Over perhaps six years of life, a harvester ant queen may lay thousands of eggs fertilized by the sperm stored in her body from that single mating frenzy. The majority of her eggs grow into sterile, wingless female ants. These generations devote their lives to tending the queen and their sisters, enlarging the nest, foraging for food, and defending the colony.

When a harvester ant colony has grown sufficiently large, the queen lays special eggs which mature into winged, fertile beings of both sexes. On summer evenings after rainstorms, the winged ants pour from their parent colony, take to the air, and cruise for mates. After the frenzy is over, mated females fly off in search of a place to dig a nest; males die. The next year, a new generation arrives to consummate their desires.

Ant colonies are excellent examples of superorganisms, groups of lives that act as if they were parts of some larger being. Altruism, cooperation for the sake of the whole group, is the corporate culture here, not independent thinking. According to Hölldobler and his colleague Edward O. Wilson, this self-sacrificial colonial existence is the reason for ants' abundance and importance on earth.

Harvester ants, as their name implies, are seed-eating ants. In clement weather—when the above-ground air temperature is between about 60 and 120 degrees—harvester ant workers stream out of their underground nests to collect seeds and leaves. These efficient foragers have an enormous impact on desert ecosystems. Workers from a single colony of harvester ants travel as far as 130 feet from their nest, and can collect as many as 7,000 seeds in a day—over 2 million seeds per year. (Each worker can lift fifty times her own weight.) Colonies often strip the vegetation around their nest for many feet. The relationship between plants and ants works both ways, however. Some desert plants, including sacred datura, rely on harvester ants to spread their seeds around. These plants have evolved seeds with alluring scents, special "handles" to make carrying easy, and tough coats that ant jaws cannot penetrate. Ants carry the seeds away from the parent plant, but abandon them uneaten.

Since harvester ants are abundant and large, it seems logical that they would be a coveted food source. But their aggressive self-defense deters most predators. A harvester ant grasps its attacker with powerful jaws, thrusts the stinger at the end of its abdomen into the attacker's skin, and injects a venom that causes excruciating pain in humans and can immobilize smaller animals.

One predator, however, has evolved ways to exploit this plentiful, but difficult, food resource. Horned lizards—small, stout lizards unique to the western parts of North and Central America—eat *only* ants, including harvester ants. Horned lizards are named for the ferocious collar of hornlike spines that rings the base of their head. Their flattened, toadlike body earns them another common name, horny toad.

Horned lizards' predilection for ants means significant tradeoffs for the little lizards. Their chosen food may be abundant, but it is low in energy, giving these lizards a sluggish metabolism. In order to obtain sufficient nutrition, horned lizards must pack away large amounts of ants, hence their tanklike body, designed to accommodate an enormous stomach, which comprises some 30 percent of their body weight. (In a 120-pound human, an analogous stomach would weigh about forty pounds!) Even the lizards' hunting behavior is affected by their prey: in order to avoid being stung, horned lizards hunt with unlizardlike stealth. A horned lizard hides by an ant foraging trail, munches a few ants, and then moves on before its prey notice it and attack. Horned lizards have also evolved antitoxins specific to harvester ant venom.

With chunky bodies and slow metabolisms, horned lizards rely on camouflage rather than speed to escape becoming dinner themselves. They can change the background color of their scales to match the shade of the soil. Dark blotches on their backs mimic shadows; fringed scales around the edges of their midsection break up their outline. Motionless, the stout lizards simply disappear. When a predator does spot one, a horned lizard calls on unusual defenses. It gulps air like a blowfish, swelling up so that its sharp "horns" make it nearly impossible to swallow. In extreme danger, a horned lizard can even squirt a stream of blood from a pore in its eyelids, startling and deterring its attacker.

Harvester ant nests are easy to locate. These ants dump their trash—waste, seed husks, small pebbles, and excavated soil—around the entrance to their nest, accumulating a cone-shaped mound. The thermal mass of the mound helps regulate both temperature and humidity inside the extensive nest. If you find a harvester ant nest, walk outwards from it in a spiral, looking closely at every small, warty rock that you see. You may find a horned lizard, waiting for a meal.

JOSHUA TREE

Palmilla
Yucca brevifolia

> *Yucca trees ... gave a strange and southern character to the country, and suited well with the dry and desert region we were approaching. Associated with the idea of barren sands, their stiff and ungraceful form makes them to the traveler the most repulsive tree in the vegetable kingdom.*
>
> —John C. Frémont (1844), quoted in WESTERN WILD FLOWERS AND THEIR STORIES

NAME: Joshua trees are named for their resemblance to the prophet Joshua. *Palmilla,* or "little palm," the plant's Spanish name, commemorates the plant's appearance. *Yucca* is the native Haitian name for these plants; *brevifolia* means short-leafed, since the bayonet-shaped leaves are shorter than those of other yuccas.

SIZE: A small tree reaching up to fifty feet high (in extraordinary individuals) with numerous shaggy, thick-trunked branches spreading up to twenty feet across.

COLOR: Flowers greenish-ivory, on stalks several feet tall

RANGE: The Mojave Desert of Southern California and southern Nevada, southwestern Utah, and the northwestern edge of the Sonoran Desert in Arizona

HABITAT: Gravely soils of *bajadas* and hillsides up to 4,000 feet elevation

Joshua trees, so the story goes, were named by Mormons traveling through the Mojave Desert in Southern California on their way to Utah. They entered a forest of the oddly shaped yucca trees and imagined that the twisting arms resembled crowds of biblical Joshuas pointing the way to the promised land.

Joshua trees are the largest yuccas in the Southwest, members of the lily family with clusters of stiff, stilettolike evergreen leaves and tall stalks of waxy flowers. Yuccas are often confused with agaves, since both bear clusters of stout leaves tipped with fierce spines and both sprout many-foot-tall stalks of flowers. Yuccas, however, bloom year after year; agaves, also called century plants, bloom but once, then die. Joshua trees bloom between February and April. The end of each shaggy branch sprouts a flower stalk laden with dense clusters of small, waxy, bell-shaped, greenish flowers. From a distance the stalks look rather like squat candles rising from weird, twisted candelabra.

In years of sufficient winter rainfall, a carpet of annual wildflowers bursts into bloom when the Joshua trees flower, briefly painting the desert landscape with vivid colors. Although the Sonoran Desert is better known for its spectacular wildflower displays, the Mojave actually boasts many more kinds of annual plants. Two hundred and fifty species of annuals—plants that sprout, bloom, reproduce, and die in the space of a season—occur in the Mojave Desert, most known only from there. In wet years, annuals sprout by the score, crowding the normally bare ground with diminutive plants in densities as high as 400 per square yard: desert gold-poppy, filaree, desert evening primrose, wing-nut forget-me-not, desert chicory, lupine, Stansbury phlox, desert gilia, and many others. Within a few weeks, as the fierce sun dries out the soil, the tiny plants desiccate and vanish without a trace (except for their seeds), leaving the ground bare again.

In some parts of the Mojave Desert, 80 percent of the plant species are annuals. The annual plant lifestyle is successful in the Mojave because this desert's average precipitation is very low, from under two to nearly eight inches per year, depending on the location, and because it is a winter-rain-only desert, receiving 65 to 98 percent of its yearly precipitation in winter. Annuals, living in the warmer environment close to the soil surface, can sprout and grow while soils remain wet, completing their whole life cycle before perennial plants "wake up" in spring.

Annual plants avoid drought by surviving as seeds, germinating only when sufficient moisture falls. Once they sprout, however, annuals are profligate consumers, squandering water in their haste to reproduce before the soil dries out. Many are tiny plants, no more than a few inches tall. They concentrate their energy in often-outsized flowers, blooming abundantly as long as their threadlike roots can pull in water. Annuals seed prolifically, producing ample quantities to feed the multitudes of desert seed-eaters with enough left to sprout colorful carpets whenever rainfall allows.

Joshua trees are the largest plants in their landscape. Their size and architecture are important to their ecosystem in various ways. Like agaves and mesquites, yuccas were once crucial sources of food and raw materials for desert-dwelling peoples. Yucca flower buds, popped off and roasted just before they bloomed, provided a seasonal sweet. The stiff leaves were soaked, pounded, or chewed to release their strong fibers, which were twisted into cords and rope to fashion everything from fishing line to animal halters, twined into baskets and sandals, and woven into mats and clothing. Yucca leaves chewed at one end are used today as delicate brushes for painting pots and pictographs. Dug up and pounded in water, the long, slender roots produce a fine, sudsy soap which is still used for ceremonial cleansings. For a short time in the late 1800s, says Charles Francis Saunders in *Western Wildflowers and Their Stories*, the woody, fibrous trunks of Joshua trees were even made into paper at a pulp mill built near Ravenna, in Southern California. The yucca-tree paper was shipped as far away as London, where several issues of the *Daily Telegraph* were printed on it. However, the high costs of shipping and the poor quality of the paper forced the mill to close. After World War I, the soft but flexible trunks were pressed into service again for splints and artificial limbs.

Joshua trees house, feed, and provide perches for desert creatures from golden eagles to termites. The lives of two Mojave Desert residents, yucca moths and yucca night lizards, are especially intimately linked to Joshua trees. Yucca moths are a group of small, drab-colored moths that have evolved a partnership with Joshua trees and other yuccas. Each species of yucca is attended by its own species of yucca moth. Yucca blossoms open at night and emit a musty smell. Lured by the scent, a female yucca moth crawls into a flower, gathers pollen, and patting the mass with her feet, works it into a tiny ball before flying to another yucca flower. She stuffs the pollen ball into the new flower's stigma, thus fertilizing it. The moth then thrusts her ovipositer into the flower's ovary, lays a few eggs and clambers out of the flower. The moth's grublike larvae feed on the yucca seeds, leaving enough uneaten to ensure a new generation of yucca. If the moth lays more eggs in any one ovary than the seed crop can support, that flower aborts and her eggs die. The two lives are inextricably intertwined: without the pollinating activities of the yucca moth, there would be no Joshua trees; without the Joshua trees, there would be no yucca moths.

Yucca night lizards, tiny, charcoal gray, velvet-skinned lizards, spend their entire lives in Joshua trees. With thin skin and lidless eyes, these several-inch-long lizards lack protection from dehydration and glaring sunlight and thus seem ill-suited for desert life. They adapt by living sedentary, nocturnal lives tucked away in the moist darkness under fallen Joshua tree trunks, eating termites and ants. Termites consume decaying Joshua tree wood, night lizards consume termites, owls and rattlesnakes consume night lizards; thus, the nutrients in Joshua trees are recycled into other desert lives.

Although nineteenth-century Mormons saw the strange, twisted figures of Joshua trees as prophets pointing the way to the promised land, early anthropologists collected a different story from the native Kawaiisu Indians, according to Charles Francis Saunders. The tree-sized yuccas, said the Kawaiisu, are enemies who were pursuing Coyote, the trickster figure in Southwest American Indian tales, and his brother. Coyote and his brother used their magic powers to halt their enemies in mid-chase, turning them into Joshua trees. But, as so often with Coyote, the magic bit back. In their terror, Coyote and his brother ran all the way to the edge of the world, said the Kawaiisu, where they turned into two stones.

Whether we label them biblical figures, "repulsive" trees, or Coyote's enemies, Joshua trees continue the slow cycles of their lives, vivid threads in the living tapestry that we call the Mojave Desert.

CURVE-BILLED THRASHER

Cuitlacoche común
Toxostoma curvirostre

> [This thrasher prefers] a habitat of thorny desert shrubs, and particularly the cholla cactus. It could well be designated as the Cholla Cactus Thrasher.
>
> —J. Stokely Ligon, NEW MEXICO BIRDS AND WHERE TO FIND THEM

NAME: Curve-billed thrashers possess long, curved bills. *Thrasher* refers to the thrashing action these birds make when they forage. *Cuitlacoche* comes from a Mexican Indian word for "songbird," and *común* means "common" in Spanish. *Toxostoma* means "bow-mouth" in Greek, *curvirostre* means "curved-bill" in Latin; both allude to the bird's bill.
SIZE: Adults grow to eleven inches long, from beak to tail tip
COLOR: Buff gray all over, with white throat and darker mottling on breast; bird's eye startlingly bright yellow or orange
RANGE: The Chihuahuan and Sonoran Deserts and adjacent arid shrublands as far north as southern Colorado, south to central México, east to the lower Rio Grande Valley of south Texas
HABITAT: Arid shrublands, especially with mesquite and cholla

"Whit-wheet!" comes the loud double-note whistle, and a robin-sized bird with a long tail flies in to land on the ground beneath a mesquite. The bird, colored the same pale gray-brown shade as the desert soil, scratches vigorously at the leaf litter under the mesquite with its long, down-curved bill. After a moment spent throwing debris around and probing the soil, the bird jerks upright, looks around with bright yellow eyes, then, seeing no immediate danger, bends to its task again.

The bird with the loud whistle is a curve-billed thrasher. Thrashers spend much of their time on the ground, running on strong, heavy legs. Like roadrunners and quail, they are as likely to run as to fly. Thrashers use their stout bills as rakes and probes to fling surface debris aside as they search out and spear small insects, spiders and other arthropods, snails, and seeds. They consume a tremendous quantity of small prey, acting as a check on soil arthropod and gastropod (snail) populations. Their vigorous digging—curve-billed thrashers excavate pits up to two inches deep in search of tasty tidbits—turns over the soil surface and plows in organic matter. When insect food is scarce, desert thrashers climb into shrubs, including cactus, to pluck and eat fruits.

Many other kinds of desert animals eat similar foods. To minimize competition, thus saving energy, would-be competitors partition the resources. The different species have evolved specializations — niches—with very little overlap. One way to partition a food resource is to forage in different physical spaces. For example, thrashers feed on the ground. Warblers glean insects from the twigs and leaves of shrubs and small trees. Woodpeckers drill into cactus and tree trunks, feeding on boring insects. Kingbirds "flycatch," catching flying insects in short aerial forays, while swallows and swifts swoop through the open air. All are desert insect-feeders, all have evolved distinct niches.

Another way to partition a resource is for would-be competitors to eat food of different sizes. For instance, thrashers and whiptail lizards, hyperactive lizards with long tails, both flick up debris from the ground to uncover insects and other arthropods. Thrashers, however, can use their strong bills to snatch prey too large for the much-smaller whiptail lizards. Animals that eat the same-sized food from the same physical space can still avoid competition by partitioning the temporal space, foraging at different times. Thrashers and scorpions, for instance, compete for some of the same types of critters, but thrashers forage during the day; scorpions scuttle over the same ground at night.

The six species of thrashers that live in western North America eat much the same food and forage in the same way at the same times of day. The ranges of the different species coincide neatly with the boundaries of the deserts and arid shrublands. Four, including the curve-billed thrasher, inhabit the hot deserts; one, the sage thrasher, summers in the cold, northerly Great Basin Desert and winters in the hot deserts; and the last lives in the dry chaparral of the southern Pacific Coast. Ornithologists—bird researchers—find that even where their ranges overlap, the six species rarely compete. Instead, they partition habitats, avoiding competition by living in different plant communities.

Curve-billed thrashers do compete for nesting space, but not with other thrashers. Their nest requirements are very specific: they prefer the armored fastness of cholla cactus. So do cactus wrens, large, harsh-voiced wrens with speckled breasts and streaked backs. Cactus wrens are serious nest-builders: a pair may build four or five dome-shaped nests in one year, one for their spring brood, one for their summer brood, and several roosting nests for protection from the harsh desert weather. Where cholla suitable for nesting are in short supply, curve-billed thrashers often destroy cactus wren roosting nests, presumably to discourage the competition.

Curve-billed thrashers raise two broods each year if conditions permit, one in spring and one in summer. Like most desert animals, curve-billed thrashers synchronize their child-rearing times to periods of moisture, when food supplies are relatively abundant. Pairs court in late winter, as early as February, and together the two build a cup-shaped nest of twigs, lined with fine grasses. The female lays two to five eggs asynchronously, one per day. Bearing young in succession, rather than at the same time, is a very common response to the unpredictable availability of food in the desert. If food is abundant, all of the young thrive. If food is scarce, the noisier and better-developed older nestlings receive more food, and the younger ones starve. This sort of natural brood reduction seems cruel, but from the point of view of the parent birds' genes, it is very practical: it allows parents to focus their feeding efforts on just a few young, raising the probability that some will survive to carry on the line, instead of all starving.

You might live in the desert a long time and never notice a curve-billed thrasher. Except for their loud, two-note whistle, these desert-colored foragers are unobtrusive birds. But their very practical solutions to partitioning the desert's sparse resources and ensuring the survival of their kind have much to teach us about life in the harsh and unpredictable conditions of North America's deserts.

TUMBLEWEED

Chamiso volador
Salsola australis

> *I'll keep rolling along,*
> *Deep in my heart is a song,*
> *Here on the range I belong,*
> *Drifting along with the tumbling tumbleweeds.*
> —Sons of the Pioneers, "Tumblin' Tumbleweeds"

NAME: Tumbleweeds do indeed tumble with the wind. *Chamiso volador* means, appropriately, "rolling shrub" in Spanish. *Salsola* comes from the Latin verb *sallere*, "to salt," referring to the salt tolerance of a seashore-dwelling relative; *australis*, "of Australia," is where the plant was originally described.

SIZE: A more-or-less spherical plant at maturity, as large as ten feet across and six feet high

COLOR: Red stems with dark green foliage when young, dries to straw color

RANGE: Native to the arid plains east of the Ural Mountains in Eurasia, introduced throughout North America, most common in the West

HABITAT: Roadsides, abandoned farmland, vacant lots, or any ground where the surface is disturbed by mechanical alteration, thus opening up new seedbeds for pioneering species.

R emember the classic Westerns—*High Noon, Shane, The Virginian?* Rolling through their scenes was a plant that has come to symbolize the American West: tumbleweed. Like the restless cowboy staying in one place only long enough to break hearts, the miner hopping from claim to claim, the farm family moving ever westward, the image of tumbleweed bounding with the wind across the landscape is a part of Western myth and legend. Ironically, tumbleweed is not a native Westerner at all. It comes from Russia's arid shrub steppes, half a world away—hence its other common name, Russian thistle.

Tumbleweed hitched a ride across the ocean with flax seed imported by Ukrainian farmers, appearing in South Dakota in the early 1870s. By 1881, the weed had bounced its way across enough of the Great Plains to come to the attention of then–U.S. Secretary of Agriculture James M. Rusk. Alarmed by reports that panic-stricken farmers were abandoning their farms, Secretary Rusk dispatched an assistant to investigate.

The report was bleak. Wherever farmers had plowed the prairies, tumbleweed took over: sprouting before their crops, drastically lowering grain yields, and interfering with harvests. The plant's sharp spines penetrated the heavy leather gloves worn by threshers and tore the flesh of draft horses. Tumbleweeds spread prairie fires and panic by rolling and leaping across fire lines, setting houses and crops ablaze. No wonder that Russian immigrants called tumbleweed "wind witch" and "leap-the-field."

Public officials proposed drastic measures to deal with the tumbling menace. One North Dakota legislator imagined building a wire fence around his state to keep tumbleweed out. New Mexico state botanist E. O. Wooton urged state residents: "Kill it all and now. . . . Never let a single plant bear seed." But this rolling bush had found niches aplenty and would not be dislodged. By the time that the Sons of the Pioneers recorded "Tumblin' Tumbleweeds" in 1934, says botanist Gary Paul Nabhan, this ubiquitous invader had made itself so at home that it symbolized the landscape and culture of the West.

Although pesticides invented after World War II keep tumbleweed from shutting down farms, today the ball-shaped plant is a fixture in arid landscapes. After winter or summer rains, bright green young plants sprout by the score on bare ground. At this stage, tumbleweed, a member of the Chenopodiaceae, or Goosefoot family, is succulent and nutritious, like its relatives, spinach and lamb's-quarters. Many desert animals—including mice, desert cottontails, quail, pronghorn antelope, and bighorn sheep—dine on the watery, nitrogen-rich shoots. (In the drought-stricken 1930s, farmers harvested young tumbleweed shoots as emergency silage for starving livestock.) But tumbleweed's tender stage is short-lived. By the time that its small, three-winged seeds are mature, it has shed its water-losing leaves, leaving behind spiny bracts, and dried into a tough, globe-shaped skeleton ranging from the size of a basketball to that of a compact car.

The plant called *chamiso volador* harnesses an abundant desert resource—wind—to pollinate its flowers and disseminate its seeds.

Its tiny blossoms loose clouds of minute pollen grains on the moving streams of air to float from flower to flower. (And, unfortunately, into the sinuses of desert-dwelling humans. Tumbleweed pollen is a major allergen in the Southwest.) As the soil dries out, a special layer of cells at the base of the plant's stem dies, creating a weak area like the abscission layer that severs the stems of the leaves on deciduous trees. Thereafter, the first good tug of wind sets tumbleweeds free to bound across the landscape, spreading their seeds far and wide.

A single tumbleweed plant produces a prodigious number of seeds—as many as a quarter of a million. Because the plant sets so many seeds in a short time, tumbleweed cannot afford to provide frills such as stored energy reserves like fruits or fancy coverings like nuts. The seeds—each simply a coiled, embryonic plant covered by a thin outer membrane—do not even possess compounds to inhibit germination. Instead, tumbleweed relies on a simple mechanism to avoid winter's killing temperatures: the infant plant spends the cold season growing and cannot germinate until it is mature. Then, unlike most seeds, which germinate slowly, cell by cell, the tumbleweed seedling is formed and ready to grow: once moisture soaks the seed cover, the plant simply uncoils, screwing its root into the soil and spreading its two slender, needle-like leaves to the sun, and spurts upward. This plant takes literally the maxim "Bloom where you are planted": the seeds can germinate in soil so salty that other plants dehydrate and die, and at temperatures ranging from 28 to 100 degrees!

When I look at tumbleweed, I think not of botany or land management, but of the word "weed" and what it means: something in the way, unwanted, not native. I am reminded of my own tumbleweed existence, bouncing around the continent from Illinois to Wyoming to West Virginia to Washington state to Colorado to Iowa, and now, snagged on a barbwire fence in New Mexico. Like tumbleweed, I am not a native of this desert landscape. Does that mean that I am a weed? I think, too, of the giant steel fence that we are erecting along *La Frontera*, the border between the United States and México, to keep "illegal aliens" out—people whose ancestors inhabited these landscapes when mine were building longboats in Norway. Who is the "alien" here? When I see tumbleweed bounding across the desert on the spring winds, I am reminded that life is by no means simple, that boundaries are never as clear as the lines drawn on a map, and that there are lessons to be learned from watching weeds.

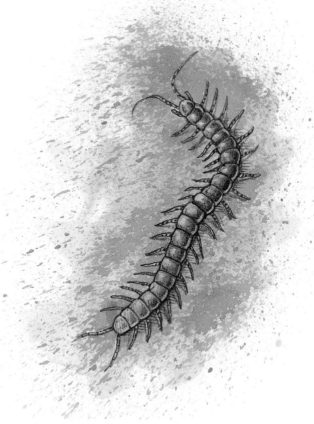

GIANT DESERT CENTIPEDE

Cienpiés
Scolopendra heros

> *After one gets over the feeling of uneasiness caused by the elongated
> bodies and numerous legs in different phases of motion, the animals are
> exceedingly interesting.*
> —Stephen Williams and Robert Hefner, "Millipedes and
> Centipedes of Ohio"

NAME: Giant desert centipedes are big and they live in the desert. *Centipede* comes from the Latin for "hundred feet." *Cienpiés*, the Spanish word for centipede, also means "hundred feet." *Scolopendra* means "centipede" in Greek; *heros* is "hero," also for this centipede's large size.
SIZE: Adults grow to nine inches long
COLOR: Desert tan with greenish black on head and hind end
RANGE: From the Chihuahuan and Sonoran desert regions south to central México
HABITAT: Shrub deserts and desert grasslands up to about 5,000 feet elevation
NOTES: These are the largest centipedes in North America. They can live two years.

I am not scared of many things. But centipedes, with their penchant for darkness, multiple legs flowing in unison, and venomous bite, give me the creeps. Still, once I get over my initial revulsion, I find these crawly creatures fascinating. Centipedes are arthropods, critters with external, jointed skeletons like insects, scorpions, or crabs. They are named for the erroneous belief that they have one hundred feet, but, in reality, centipedes rarely possess more than 70 legs (and never less than 30). *Cienpiés* are commonly confused with similarly multilegged millipedes, but the two are quite distinct: centipedes' bodies are flattened; millipedes' are rounded and wormlike. Centipedes sprout one pair of legs per body segment, millipedes, two pairs. Even their diet differs. Millipedes graze on plant material; centipedes eat meat. (Millipede, meaning "thousand feet" in Latin, is another exaggeration. Early naturalists apparently had difficulty counting those wriggling extremities!)

Like all arthropods, *cienpiés* wear their skeletons on their sleeves, growing a hard outer shell instead of an internal frame. But unlike most creatures with exoskeletons, centipedes' body armor is quite elastic. Their flexible shell allows them to easily deform their body in order to gallop across open ground, burrow quickly beneath a rock, or squeeze into a tight crevice. Such extraordinary elasticity, however, means that their body armor is thin and skimpy: in fact, it affords little protection from dehydration. Exposed to the desert's thirsty air, centipedes desiccate quickly.

In order to avoid dehydrating, giant desert centipedes hunt in the cooler, more humid hours of night, spending the day buried under rocks or wood. (Centipedes are thigmotactic—oh, lovely word!— able to rest only when most of their body is touching something solid.) During extreme hot and dry spells, giant desert centipedes retreat into other animals' underground burrows and become dormant until the rains bring more humid weather.

Living in darkness, centipedes depend on keen tactile and olfactory senses. Their segmented antennae "smell" odors, and help centipedes feel their way, locate prey, and measure humidity. In addition, most *cienpiés'* trailing last pair of legs also serve as antennalike sensors, guiding them when they back up in tight spaces. Some species also "see" in darkness with sensory organs and sensitive hairs on their feet.

Giant desert centipedes are active hunters. Once one spots a potential meal, it runs swiftly towards the prey, its multiple legs running with a curious undulating motion. The *cienpiés* quickly grasps the animal with whatever legs are handy and administers the coup de grace with a quick pinch of its poison claws, a pair of sickle-shaped, venom-dispensing pincers at the end of its first pair of legs. Such "bites" paralyze small creatures, but are usually no more painful than a bee or wasp sting to humans. Giant desert centipedes can and do dispatch prey larger than themselves, including lizards, geckos, toads, snakes, and rodents. In *The Biology of Centipedes*, J.G.E. Lewis tells of watching a 3¾-inch-long giant desert centipede dragging away a freshly killed, ten-inch-long snake!

The courtship of such crawly, sensitive, venomous hunters is a touchy affair. How does an amorous centipede let his intended (males usually initiate courtship) know that he is a suitor, not a meal? He approaches her cautiously and disarms her by grasping her poison claws with a pair of his legs—but sometimes, despite his circumspection, he still ends up as dinner. (Tarantula spider males and scorpion males are similarly wary in their approach, for similar reasons.) The male *cienpiés* may then spend hours rhythmically tapping the female with his antennae and legs before consummating the relationship: he deposits a packet of sperm on the ground and carefully maneuvers her over to where she can suck it into her genital opening.

Days or weeks later, the female giant desert centipede lays a clutch of a dozen or more eggs, then wraps her length around them. For the next month, until the eggs hatch, the mother centipede turns her eggs and licks them frequently to keep them from drying out (they die if the relative humidity drops to 3 percent, not unusual in the desert) and to prevent fungal infection. After the eggs hatch, the mother feeds and tends the young *cienpiés* for about a month, until they have grown large enough to survive on their own.

Centipedes and millipedes are commonly confused, but the two many-legged creatures live very different lives. Desert millipedes spend at least three-fourths of each year underground in other animals' burrows. After surfacing, these slow-moving, mahogany brown crawlers rehydrate their bodies by eating moist soil or taking up water anally. Desert millipedes are grazers, chewing up dead leaves, shrub and tree bark, and other plant material. Their recycling keeps organic material moving through environments so dry that rot is rare. Despite their size—up to seven inches long—and succulent flesh, most predators avoid desert millipedes, repelled by smelly vapor emitted by pairs of repugnatorial glands located behind each of their many pairs of legs. Only one small insect, the wormlike, luminescent larvae of the *Zarrhipis* beetle, devours desert millipedes, apparently undeterred by their stink.

Strolling up a desert road one moonless night, I spotted what looked like a tiny, glowing ember on the roadside—only the light was green, not orange. It was far too dark to discern the outline of the *Zarrhipis* larvae, but bending close, I saw its luminescence pulse rhythmically, like the beating of a heart. Watching that tiny pulsing light, I understood the connection that unites all beings: whether predator or prey, grazer or grazed, human or tiny beetle larvae —we all pulse with life, impelled by the same basic desires.

BURROWING OWL

Lechuza llanera
Speotyto cunicularia

The "ground owl" is quite distinct in every way from the other owls and so has a separate name in most Pueblo languages. Burrowing owls' [appearance] ... coupled with the habit of nodding and bobbing the whole body, combines to produce a priest or a clown—which in Pueblo terms may be the same.

—Hamilton A. Tyler, PUEBLO BIRDS AND MYTHS

NAME: Burrowing owls live in burrows. *Lechuza llanera* means "owl of the plains" in Spanish. *Speotyto* means "cave-dwelling owl" in Greek; *cunicularia* is Latin for "burrower" or "miner."

SIZE: Nine to eleven inches long with a wingspread of up to two feet

COLOR: Back, wings, and upper parts brown with buff white spots; lower parts are the reverse, buff white with brown barring

RANGE: The western Americas from western Canada south through Central America and, locally, to Tierra del Fuego, also dry grasslands in southern Florida and several Caribbean islands

HABITAT: Dry grasslands and deserts, as well as irrigation ditchbanks, cemeteries, university campuses, airports, and other artificial shortgrass "prairies"

A burrowing owl standing at the entrance of its hole on long legs does indeed bring to mind a diminutive elder or a stumpy clown as it turns its earless, flattop head around backwards to watch passers-by, then bows and chatters as noisily as a prairie dog. Burrowing owls are oddities in the owl world. Typically, owls hunt at night and spend the daylight hours roosting in trees; most species inhabit forests and woodlands. Burrowing owls, however, inhabit treeless deserts and grasslands and dwell in holes in the ground. Further, these contrary owls are just as likely to be out hunting in bright daylight as at night.

On spring afternoons, I often see a burrowing owl standing at the entrance of its burrow, scanning the nearby ditchbank for prey. I have to look hard to see the owl: the spotted pattern of its brown and cream plumage blends beautifully into the dotted shadow pattern of desert shade. But then it moves, looking like a wizened gnome on long legs. As I pass on the ditch road, the *lechuza's* big yellow eyes follow me without blinking, its head swiveling, swiveling, and swiveling, until it has rotated nearly backwards. If I come too close, the little owl bows—dipping its body by bending its legs—and clacks its bill at me, then silently vanishes underground.

Vanishing underground is distinctly unowllike behavior. But it is a very practical solution for owls that inhabit ecosystems where trees are scarce. By appropriating and enlarging abandoned burrows dug by prairie dogs and other animals, burrowing owls gain shelter from the heat and aridity, as well as protection from some predators. (In the deserts and grasslands of the West, perhaps because of the abundance of burrowing animals, these *lechuzas* rarely dig their own burrows. Their association with prairie dogs is so close, in fact, that the Zuñi Indians call burrowing owls "priests of the prairie dogs.") Burrowing owls have also adopted human-created habitats that mimic their preferred grassland habitat, including golf course margins, cemeteries, city parks, and airports. On the university campus near where I live, they "burrow" in the downspouts of buildings!

Although these small *lechuzas* are somewhat contrary to the prevalent owl mode, they share basic characteristics with other owls. Their eyes, for instance, are designed for night vision, like those of all owls. Owls' eyes are large relative to the size of their bodies, and possess a high proportion of light-gathering rods. And, like other owls, burrowing owls possess specially modified flight feathers, allowing them to fly in complete silence and to hunt using the element of surprise.

Burrowing owls are opportunistic feeders: that is, they eat just about any animal that they can catch, including insects, centipedes, scorpions, mice and other small rodents, lizards, frogs, toads, and even small birds. They often hunt by hovering above open areas and then dropping, powerful feet outstretched, on their intended meal. Or they flycatch, snatching insects out of the air. Unlike other owls, burrowing owls also catch their food on foot, walking, hopping, or running along the ground.

Each spring, these gnomelike owls appear in the deserts and dry grasslands across western North America to breed and raise young. Males arrive first. They stake a claim to a burrow that suits them, clean out last year's debris and enlarge it. When females arrive, they check out the real estate, and, ornithologists say, probably pick mates by the desirability of the burrow that they offer. (For this species at least, househusbandly talents do pay!) A male burrowing owl attracts a female by flying up over the burrow entrance, circling, then hovering overhead. If a female responds, he lands and the two stand atop the burrow and quietly call to each other. They cross bills, preen each other, and stretch their wings together in balletlike moves. He offers her a piece of food. Then he stretches himself upwards, standing as tall as he can, and displays white facial patches. If his intended is receptive, she responds by also displaying her facial patches. Then he mounts her in a musical copulation: he warbles and coos; she sings a series of down-slurred notes.

After mating, the pair excavates a nest chamber deep in the burrow, kicking dirt backwards and out of the burrow with their powerful feet. *Lechuzas* usually line the nest with manure, probably to disguise the smell of their toothsome young. The female then lays a huge clutch of eggs — as many as a dozen. Ground-nesting animals often birth large broods to compensate for the extra-high predation. Badgers and domestic dogs dig out burrowing owl burrows; skunks, ferrets, Gila monsters, and snakes crawl right into the holes to eat the eggs and young; hawks circle overhead to snatch unwary birds.

Burrowing owls are born helpless and with their eyes closed. Their mother, who rarely leaves the burrow, is the primary caregiver; their father provides food. Young burrowing owls are very vocal. Besides an "eep!" of alarm and a rasping begging call, they make a rattling sound very like that of an alert rattlesnake, leading to a folktale that *lechuzas* and rattlers share burrows. They don't, but the sound undoubtedly deters some predators. The owlets leave their natal burrow and forage on their own at about two months old. By fall, they are ready to fly south with the adult burrowing owls to winter as far south as northern South America.

Come the next year, these young *lechuzas* reappear, ready to stake their claim to a burrow of their own, hoping to attract a mate and bless the desert with another brood of chattering, curious, contrary, ground-dwelling owls.

RAZORBACK SUCKER

Matalote jorobado
Xyrauchen texanus

> Dams do literally kill rivers,... not only living water and natural scenery but a whole congeries of values associated with them.
> —Wallace Stegner, THE AMERICAN WEST AS LIVING SPACE

NAME: Named for their keeled back, shaped like the blade of a straight razor. *Matalote* is a Spanish name for "sucker"; *jorobado* means "hump-backed." *Xyrauchen* means "razor-neck," *texanus* is a misnomer, as this fish is native to the Colorado River of the Southwest, not of Texas.

SIZE: Adults grow to three feet long and weigh up to fifteen pounds

COLOR: Olive- to brown-black above, brown or pink sides, yellow to white below; breeding males turn orange below with rosy fins

RANGE: Once swam in all of the medium to large rivers of the Colorado River system, from Wyoming and Colorado to Baja California; now only above the Grand Canyon and in Lakes Mead, Mohave, and Havasu on the lower Colorado

HABITAT: Silt- to rock-bottomed backwaters near strong current and deep pools in medium to large rivers; also impoundments

NOTES: Razorback suckers can live as long as fifty years.

In the late 1600s, Father Eusebio Francisco Kino visited the Indians living along the Gila River near present-day Phoenix, Arizona, on a mission to save their souls. In his diary, Kino mentioned with surprise these desert-dwellers' diet, which included an abundance of fish of many kinds.

Fish are not part of our usual image of the desert. Indeed, when the sun blazes hot and the only water in sight proves to be the shimmer of a mirage, it is hard to imagine water existing in these sere landscapes at all, much less enough of the liquid to support fish. But the desert's rivers once spawned a plentiful variety of fish, from six-foot-long Colorado squawfish to tiny Gila topminnows. In fact, desert fish were so abundant that, in the late 1800s, commercial fisherman hawked fresh catches of razorback suckers, squawfish, shovel-nosed sturgeon, and humpback and buffalo chub on the streets of boomtowns from Bisbee and Phoenix to Albuquerque and El Paso.

Dozens of fish species are native to the North American deserts, and most are endemic—that is, they live nowhere else. Indeed, many species are found in just one river system, or only one stream or spring. Why so many species with such limited distribution? A combination of geological forces and climate long ago isolated these once-wider-ranging fish, causing them to evolve into place-specific, distinct species.

Beginning around 150 million years ago, the Sierra Nevada and the Cascade Range were pushed up by the continuing collision of two crustal plates: the expanding Pacific Ocean crust and the North American continent. Partially blocked from the supply of Pacific Ocean moisture by these new, high mountain ranges, the inner continent gradually dried out, growing more and more desertlike. Over the millennia, the fish in the remaining desert rivers and streams — increasingly isolated by an ever-more arid landscape—either adapted to the specific local conditions or died out. Those that survived are unique and uniquely shaped by the conditions of their home river, stream, or spring. One of the most extreme examples of this tight evolutionary fit between fish and river is the razorback sucker, found nowhere else in the world but the Colorado River drainage.

Imagine a big fish, growing up to three feet long at maturity, with a body flattened from side to side to the sleek slenderness of a racing sailboat. Behind the fish's head rises what looks like an upside-down, scale-covered keel: its back kinks upward in a high, narrow protuberance the shape of an old-fashioned straight razor. Its head is blunt, with a forward bulge and a small, underslung mouth sporting thick, warty lips. A razorback sucker looks like a caricature of a fish made from ill-assorted spare parts.

This peculiar-looking body, however, is perfectly designed to survive in the fish's chosen habitat: the fastwater reaches of the Colorado River system. Razorback suckers' flattened shape and knife-thin back hump act as a keel, helping them stay oriented with a minimum amount of energy in the turbulence of roaring spring floods. That sloping forehead pushes their heads downward, so that these fish can easily hug the river bottom where they feed. Thick lips help them feel their way along river-bottom rocks; the suction created by their tiny mouth opening allows them to vacuum fly and mosquito larvae, algae, and other food from the rocks. Their small eyes are an adaptation to murky water: razorback suckers "see" as much with smell, taste, and their awareness of varying water pressure as with vision. Even the razorback sucker's small, deeply-embedded scales are tuned to fastwater habitat, designed to reduce the friction and drag of water rushing past the fish's body.

Before dams blocked their passage, razorback suckers once swam the entire length of the Colorado River, embarking on long spawning migrations in late winter and spring when water levels and temperatures rise. Razorback suckers spawn along river shorelines and in bays with gravely substrates, where water depths range from one to eighteen feet, and temperatures from 65 to 75 degrees. While a female sucker lays eggs in a sticky mass in the water, a male rushes in, grasps her with special hooked fins, and squirts his sperm over her egg mass. The fertilized egg masses drift along the bottom and eventually catch and adhere. The tiny fish that hatch later can live to be forty or fifty years old—if they can evade the mouths of hungry predators, and survive the extremes of both flood and drought that characterize their desert river.

Razorback suckers were important enough to Indians of the lower Colorado River basin that they had their own names: the Yuman called them *tsa'xnap*, the Cocopah, *suxyex*. Their bones are common in archeological sites, as are the remains of special V-shaped fishing weirs built to catch these big, tasty fish. Even after European settlement, razorback suckers were so abundant in the lower river basin that farmers speared barrowloads of them with pitchforks and used them to fertilize their fields. Now these keel-backed fish are on the endangered species list, along with dozens of other species of desert fish.

What happened? Beginning in the early twentieth century, dams "tamed" the wild Colorado and most other desert rivers, drastically altering fish habitat, throwing a wrench into the finely tuned evolutionary works of river and fish. Gone is the flush of relatively warm, sediment- and nutrient-rich water of spring and summer floods.

Gone is the scour-and-deposit rhythm that maintained spawning and feeding habitat. Today's Colorado is largely a chain of reservoirs ponded behind dams, offering plenty of habitat for lake-dwelling fish, but little for river-dwellers. Below each dam emerges a river more like a mountain stream than a desert flood: the water is cold, coming from the bottom of the reservoir, and clear. Too, its flow is regulated by the needs of irrigators and power consumers, not by seasonal rhythms basic to the lives of desert fish. In addition, irrigation withdrawals have, in places, sucked whole rivers dry. Channelization to prevent floods has altered river flow and bottom habitat. Introduced game fish species—such as bass—eat young native fish, including razorback suckers.

The bounty of desert fish that so astonished European explorers is gone from the rivers, and from our collective memory. Few desert-dwellers even see the possibility of fish and free-running rivers and streams. Our short-sightedness impoverishes these landscapes. Can we learn to live in a way that leaves room for farms *and* fish, for hydropower dams *and* spring floods? We must, I think, if we are to survive. The stories of razorback suckers and other desert fish carry lessons that we need to hear. A desert without its fish and rivers is not fit for humans, either.

SAGUARO

Pitahaya
Carnegia gigantea

> *Standing sentinel in the forbidding desert wastes, the saguaro consti-*
> *tutes a grand, green answer to our oldest question, What are Life's*
> *chances against Death?*
> —Frederick Turner, OF CHILES, CACTI, AND FIGHTING
> COCKS

NAME: Saguaro is the Spanish version of *sa-wa-ro*, an Indian name for the cactus. *Pitahaya* is from the Tohono O'odham (Papago) word for both saguaros and organ pipe cactus. *Carnegia* honors Andrew Carnegie, whose fortune endowed the first institute devoted to studying the North American deserts; *gigantea*, "giant" in Greek, refers to the size of this cactus.

SIZE: A single-trunked cactus up to forty feet tall with a straight, fluted trunk and heavy, curving arms

COLOR: Trunk and arms pale green; flowers creamy white

RANGE: Below 4,000 feet elevation in the Sonoran Desert in southern and western Arizona, adjacent northwestern México, and southeastern California

HABITAT: Grows on the well-drained soils of the *bajadas* and hillsides

NOTES: The saguaro cactus is Arizona's state flower. Saguaros can live as long as 175 years.

When we think "desert," many of us picture a landscape punctuated by the tall, semaphore-armed figures of the saguaro cactus. This giant cactus is, as Frederick Turner says in *Of Chiles, Cacti, and Fighting Cocks,* "the generic cactus that stands for the life of all those lands 'out there' in the West." Yet saguaros are restricted to just one part of the American West, the Sonoran Desert, and they only inhabit part of that area.

No wonder, though, that they have become a popular symbol of the desert: Saguaros' stately trunks tower over surrounding desert vegetation, rising three stories high and bearing a dozen or more arms. They are, simply, awesome. Weighing as much as several tons, saguaros are one of North America's two largest species of cacti; only the *cardón*, or elephant cactus, of México is larger. More than just big, however, saguaros are graceful as well, their fluted stems standing ramrod-straight on surprisingly narrow bases, their heavy arms curving upwards as if saluting the blue desert sky.

Saguaros grow painfully slowly, taking many decades to reach their massive mature size. Like all cacti, saguaros have traded fast growth rates for sophisticated ways to thrive in the extreme aridity and high solar radiation of desert environments: they abandoned leaves, growing non-photosynthesizing spines instead; they evolved a thick, waxy coating over their delicate skin tissue; and they adopted a method of photosynthesizing that allows them to only open their pores in the cooler, moister nighttime. These adaptations give cacti crucial protection from water loss and sunburn, but drastically reduce their rate of food production and thus, growth. A saguaro grows so slowly that it may spend its first ten years to grow just a few inches tall! To reach fifteen feet in height takes one of these giants from sixty to 100 years, depending on local conditions.

Saguaros' eventual massive size presents serious architectural and engineering problems. The first is water. How can such a large plant obtain and store enough water to survive the desert's long months of drought? Many desert plants store water in the more clement environment of the soil, in swollen taproots or fleshy root networks. (So abundant, in fact, are the roots of desert plants that my great-grandfather, Dr. William A. Cannon, who studied them, used to say that if the sparse vegetation of the desert were turned upside-down and the roots exposed, it would look pretty much like a jungle.) But cacti don't store water in their roots. Instead, they use the above-ground part of their body as a water reservoir. A saguaro trunk is a living sponge of succulent storage tissue, protected by a waxy outer skin and held up by a ring of rodlike vertical ribs running from the cactus's base to the tip of its trunk and arms. A mature saguaro can store as much as a ton of water—nearly doubling its empty weight. A shallow, skirtlike network of roots extending out as far as 100 feet from the trunk takes in water from even the slightest rain.

Taking up and storing a ton or more of water in a vertical column resting on a base twelve inches or so in diameter calls for creative engineering. The saguaro's fluted trunk allows the cactus to expand

and contract without tearing the waxy outer skin—the pleats in the trunk simply grow shallower as the cactus takes up water, and deeper as it uses its stores. A saguaro's stem may swell for several weeks after heavy rains and then shrink slowly for months. The semi-detached ribs—one per trunk ridge—provide a flexible, but strong, column of support. However, saguaros haven't solved one life-threatening problem: windthrow. Once full of water, saguaros are top-heavy. Lacking anchoring taproots, the giant cacti may topple in the gusts that sweep across the desert during summer thunderstorms. In fact, the taller and larger the saguaro, the greater its chances of death from windthrow.

This problem intrigues evolutionary biologist John Alcock. Why, he asks in *Sonoran Desert Spring*, would a saguaro invest so much energy and time in growing tall if the risk of toppling in the wind also increases? Because the taller the saguaro, says Alcock, the better chance the giant cactus has of successfully reproducing.

Saguaros reach a height of at least six feet before they put energy into reproduction. When they do, they put on quite a show. Dozens of knobby buds sprout at the end of their stems and open on May and June nights, revealing three-inch-wide, waxy white flowers filled with thousands of golden stamens. The blossoms attract flocks of nectar-feeders, including long-nosed bats, the giant cactus's principal pollinator. A long-nosed bat hovers above a saguaro flower and pushes its whole head into the blossom to slurp nectar with its tongue. When it emerges, the bat's fur is dusted with golden pollen, which it carries as it flies on to the next flower and the next, cross-pollinating each blossom that it visits. The taller the saguaro, thinks Alcock, the better the chances that these night-flying bats—which rely on sight, rather than sonar—can spot the flowers in the dark. It is an elegant trade: the saguaros provide high-energy nectar and high-protein pollen to fuel the bats' hovering flight; the bats provide genetic courier services, carrying pollen from plant to plant.

Alcock suggests that growing tall may also help saguaros distribute their seeds. The scarlet-fleshed, sweet, and juicy fruits, each the size of a child's fist and containing thousands of tiny black seeds, ripen in July. Only winged insects, birds, and people bearing long poles can reach the fruit, situated at the top of the tall stems. Birds, according to Alcock—primarily curve-billed thrashers and white-winged doves—are the most important saguaro seed-dispersers. They fly far from the parent plant before depositing the seeds—encased in a pat of fertilizer—under the very nurse trees that saguaros require for their survival. Saguaro seedlings cannot make it through their first few decades of life without the shade and protection from freezing temperatures provided by the canopies of small desert trees such as palo verde and ironwood. As a giant cactus grows, however, its spreading root system may outcompete that of its nurse, killing the very tree that nurtured it.

Saguaros stand tall in terms of their importance to desert ecosystems as well. These giant cacti fill the niche of big trees, providing nesting platforms for large birds, including red-tail and Harris's hawks, and great horned owls. Gila woodpeckers and gilded flickers excavate nest holes in the cacti's fleshy stems. Once abandoned, these holes provide shelter for many other birds, including tiny elf owls and ash-throated flycatchers. The flowers and fruit feed a plethora of desert consumers, from insects to humans. So important are saguaros to the desert-dwelling Tohono O'odham, in fact, that the O'odham new year officially begins when saguaro fruits ripen. The Tohono O'odham gather the ripe saguaro fruits by knocking them down carefully with poles and call down the summer rains by drinking wine fermented from the sweet fruits. Saguaros, say the Tohono O'odham, are sacred and should be treated with respect; they are people, they say, like us.

The Sonoran Desert without saguaros is unthinkable. Yet, in Arizona, mature saguaros are dying faster than new ones are becoming established. Some scientists fear that in a hundred years saguaros will have disappeared from the northern end of their range in Arizona. And no one knows why. For all we know about the desert, many questions remain unanswered.

SUMMER

"Hell season!" exclaims a geologist friend of mine, referring to summer in the desert. No matter which desert, summers are hot—extremely hot. Midday temperatures at the lower elevations reach into the hundreds, the hundred-teens in the southern deserts. Such heat can be deadly, especially for humans. Wear a hat and sun protection, and carry plenty of water. And learn from the desert's residents: take to the shade or go indoors for a *siesta*—a nap—during the hottest parts of the day. The best times to be out are during the cooler hours of morning and evening, when animals emerge and set about the business of life.

Summer differs dramatically across the deserts' enormous geographic range and, just as abruptly, but on a more local scale, across elevational ranges. Average air temperatures cool about 4 degrees for every thousand feet of elevation gain; thus, as you go uphill the climate becomes more northerly. For instance, when it is 108 degrees at midday in my backyard at 3,800 feet elevation, atop the rocky mountain peaks nearby, it is a positively pleasant 88 degrees, more like summer in Montana than the Chihuahuan Desert. (A rule of thumb says that for each 5,000 feet of elevation gain, the climate change is equivalent to going 1,500 miles northward.) Too, mountain ranges harvest more rain, as the air rising to pass over them cools, forcing its moisture to condense and fall as rain or snow. The combination of cooler average temperatures and more moisture makes desert mountain ranges verdant "islands," home to species that cannot survive in the hot, arid expanses below.

Summer brings much-needed warmth and thus green to much of

the Great Basin Desert, with its northern winters and cool, high elevations. In contrast, summer is the hottest, driest time in the adjacent Mojave Desert, which rarely receives summer rain. As air temperatures heat up in the Mojave in late spring and early summer, the soils dry to dust and the plants become dormant. Animals either reduce their activity or move away. But to the east in the similarly hot Sonoran and Chihuahuan Deserts, summer brings rain in the form of thunderstorms, and thus, renewed life. Locals in these deserts jokingly call summer "monsoon season," for the high humidity and floods these storms bring.

The summer thunderstorms are glorious events: often sudden, usually brief, and full of Wagnerian *sturm und drang*. They are also dangerous. These storms can be quite violent, flooding the desert with several inches of rain, filling normally dry arroyos and washes bank-to-bank in minutes with roaring brown slurry. Never camp, hike in, or try to drive across a wash or arroyo after a thunderstorm, or if you can see storm clouds up-drainage. One of the ironies of this intensely arid country is that drowning in such flash floods is a common cause of death. The lightning that comes with summer storms can be fatal, as well—in fact, lightning is the desert's deadliest weather phenomenon, killing several people every year.

Summer is butterfly and moth season. Wherever rain has fallen, local insect populations explode to feed on the temporary vegetative abundance. In daytime, the air is full of fluttering butterflies, as if the flowers themselves had taken wing. As dusk falls, butterflies retire and moths take over, humming through the cooler air in search of flower nectar and pollen. Look for these insects wherever wildflowers bloom in dense patches, from mountain canyons to wet spots in sand dunes.

Most desert animals time their breeding to the warm-season rains, so that they are feeding young when food is abundant. Look for babies of all sorts in summer, from beetles and lizards to quail and pronghorn antelope.

Couch's Spadefoot Toad

Sapo de espuela
Scaphiopus couchii

> "How does a toad get into the middle of the desert?" I wanted to know. "Does it rain toad frogs in Arizona?"
>
> "They're here all along, smarty. Burrowed in the ground. They wait out the dry months kind of deadlike, just like everything else, and when the rain comes they wake up and crawl out of the ground and start to holler."
>
> —Barbara Kingsolver, THE BEAN TREES

NAME: Spadefoot refers to the black, hard-edged scraper on these toads' hind feet that they use for digging. *Sapo de espuela*, in Spanish, means "spurred toad." *Scaphiopus* means "hollowed-out foot" in Greek; Couch is the person for whom the toad was named.

SIZE: 2½ to 3½ inches from snout to tail nub at maturity

COLOR: Adults greenish gold and marked with black blotches; tadpoles black

RANGE: The hottest, driest parts of the deserts and the Great Plains, from southwest Oklahoma and southeastern California to San Luis Potosí, México

HABITAT: Mesquite shrublands, creosote bush desert, shortgrass plains, and thornforest, wherever the soil is loose and easy to dig in

NOTES: Their wailing cries sound like a distant flock of bleating sheep. Various species of spadefoot toads—each with a distinctive voice—are found throughout the deserts.

In summer, after months of increasingly hot and parched weather, moist air masses sweep over the southern deserts. Fluffy cumulus clouds build and coalesce into towering thunderheads. Cold gusts of wind sweep across the desert, cloud bellies burst open, and curtains of water pour down, accompanied by brilliant stabs of lightning and booming crashes of thunder. The storms dissipate as quickly as they form, leaving the land splattered with temporary puddles and ponds. The brief abundance of water triggers the emergence of many desert lives, including spadefoot toads.

Spadefoot toads, small creatures with big voices, appear as if by magic. Before the rains, the desert is toadless. After the thunderstorms, these *sapitos*—little toads—are everywhere. When the puddles and ponds created by the rain vanish, so do the toads. Their sudden appearance and equally sudden disappearance is one of the desert's miracles.

Spadefoot toads are amphibians, creatures with Dr. Jekyll–Mr. Hyde lives: from egg through their brief life as tadpoles, they are aquatic beings, unable to survive out of water; at sexual maturity, they metamorphose into lunged, terrestrial creatures. Even out of water, they still need it: their spongelike, porous skin offers no protection against dehydration. Exposed to the desert air, these *sapitos* dry as hard as old leather in a few hours. Still, spadefoots live in the open desert, far from permanent water. In fact, Couch's spadefoots have been found in parts of the Mojave Desert where two years may pass without rain. What magic allows them to survive?

Sapitos do exactly what Barbara Kingsolver's character says: they burrow into the ground, burying themselves. There, insulated from the extremes of temperature and drought, spadefoots wait out the dry times. These little toads can dig as deep as three feet down and live for as long as two years underground, barely respiring, dormant. (They are essentially hibernating, except that hibernation implies dormancy just for the winter; *sapitos* stay underground most of the year.) Spadefoots spend the majority of their lives thus buried, in solitary exile, waiting for their night in the rain. They emerge only for short periods each year—summer in the hot deserts, spring in the Great Basin—when environmental signals predict water in brief abundance.

As the soil warms up in spring, *sapitos* gradually work their way upwards to a resting position close to the surface. There they wait, until summoned by the vibrations of thunder. *Sapitos* emerge driven by three needs: water, food, and reproduction. Water comes first. Since spadefoots do not drink—instead absorbing water directly through a porous skin patch in their bellies—a spadefoot simply hops to the nearest rain-filled puddle and squats, immersing its parched body. Once its thirst is sated, a *sapito* turns to sex. Finding a puddle large and deep enough to sustain tadpoles, a male plops in, puffs out his translucent throat, and bellows his desire; the curious trills and bleats of thousands of tiny swelling throats carry for miles. Females, drawn to the din, hop in and scull towards the sound. Their courtship is swift and wet: he clambers atop her while she floats and, holding her firmly with sticky toe pads, squirts sperm over the eggs she exudes.

Food comes in the form of swarms of flying termites and ants, also summoned from underground by the rain. When a termite or ant colony reaches sufficient size, the queen lays a special batch of eggs that hatch into reproductives, a winged generation able to reproduce. On summer nights after rains, reproductives exit their parent colony and fly off in great swarms to mate and found new colonies. After mating, females light on the ground, break their wings off, and explore for a good place to dig a nest burrow. The males, having accomplished their purpose in life—sorry, guys!—die soon after.

If a spadefoot toad surfaces at the same time and in the same place as a termite or ant mating flight, the *sapito* has hit the jackpot, the feast to end all feasts. Termite reproductives are the toad equivalent of Dove ice cream bars. Scientists analyzing the nutritional content of insects found that reproductives contain more fat and calories than some 200 other species of insects, yielding more energy per unit weight. Spadefoot toads gorge themselves on the succulent insects, eating as much as half their body weight in one night's feeding. A male Couch's spadefoot feeding on termite reproductives can, by filling his capacious stomach only once, provision himself for a year underground. (An egg-producing female must gorge herself similarly for two or three nights.) Imagine eating half of your weight in one massive feast, then digging into the ground and becoming comatose for the next year!

At dawn, the *fiesta* is over, and the dry reality of the desert sends *sapitos* back underground. They dig themselves into the soil with their "spades," black, sharp-edged scrapers on the underside of each hind leg. A digging toad seems to swim backwards into the soil, wiggling from side to side as each powerful hind foot alternately pushes dirt outwards. As the upper layers of the soil dry out, spadefoots dig themselves deeper and deeper to wait until summoned again by reverberating thunder.

Left behind in rainwater puddles and ponds are the fruits of their hurried mating. The eggs hatch within twenty-four hours into hordes of tiny, black tadpoles. These aquatic wrigglers eat plants, small aquatic animals—and sometimes each other, driven by hunger and the race to mature into air-breathing adults before their ephemeral aquatic world dries up. Couch's spadefoots are the quarter-horses of the amphibian world, sprinting from egg to adult in just over a week! (By comparison, bullfrog tadpoles take two leisurely *years*.) Surviving spadefoots emerge from their puddle, gulping air and still dragging their tail, and swim backwards into the earth.

To hear the swelling nighttime chorus of spadefoot toads is to know joy. When I hear *sapitos*, I am overcome with the urge to dance barefoot in puddles, to throw my arms wide and drink in raindrops, to celebrate the return of water to this parched land. Fortunately for urban dwellers like me, *sapitos* are not purists about their habitat. Their curious bleating and trilling calls resound from trash-filled stormwater retention basins, from roadside puddles, and from rainwater pools in vacant lots, as well as from the open desert. Their voices call us home.

OCOTILLO

Ocotillo
Fouquieria splendens

[O]n Wednesday .75 in. of rain fell in less than half an hour. When I went down the mountain after it the water rushing down sounded like a cataract.... As a result of this the plants on the hill are booming. The ocotillo began to come into leaf on Friday, the creosote bush is green again and the cacti are swollen and are brittle and easily broken.

—Dr. William A. Cannon, in a letter to Dr. D. T. MacDougal, May 19, 1904

NAME: Ocotillo is from the Aztec *ocotl,* the name for a pine with very resinous wood often used for torches; dried ocotillo stems can be used similarly, hence the Spanish *ocotillo,* or "little pine." *Fouquieria* honors French professor of medicine Pierre E. Fouquier; *splendens,* or "splendid," describes the scarlet flower clusters at the branch tips.
SIZE: A cluster of thorny stems, each up to fifteen feet tall and three inches in diameter
COLOR: Bark gray to yellow green and waxy; flowers bright scarlet; leaves small and pale green
RANGE: Below 5,000 feet elevation from west Texas to Southern California and south into México, north as far as the very tip of southern Nevada
HABITAT: Rocky desert hillsides on well-drained soil

When my great-grandfather, William Austen Cannon, moved to Tucson, Arizona, in September 1903 to found the Desert Botanical Laboratory of the Carnegie Institute, ocotillo was one of the first plants that sparked his interest. On October 23, 1903, he wrote to his mentor, Dr. D. T. MacDougal of the New York Botanical Garden:

"*Fouquieria* is interesting because it responds so delicately to its surroundings. I am told that a very little encouragement in the way of rain in the summer is sufficient to make it send out the leaves, and that it does this in a surprisingly short time after the storm."

For most of the year, ocotillo looks fearsomely dry and spiny. Its slender, gray green stems are bare but for a regular pattern of stout, inch-long thorns. The whiplike stems sprout stiffly from the base in a clump and often kink abruptly as they grow, looking like so many buggy whips in mid-crack, hence another common name, coach whip.

But as my great-grandfather discovered, ocotillo does indeed respond "delicately" to its surroundings. When the warm-season rains come, ocotillo transforms itself almost instantly. Within twelve hours after sufficient rain, tiny leaf buds dot the formerly bare stems; after twenty-four hours, the stems are covered with a dense fuzz of new, tender green leaves, making the plants look just like clumps of over-sized, bright green pipe cleaners. While the soil remains moist enough for its network of roots to absorb water, ocotillo lives wan-tonly, producing food, transpiring water, and growing new cells at a frenzied pace. As soon as the soil dries out, however, ocotillo's leaves turn yellow and fall off. The plant rests until the next rain.

One May, my great-grandfather measured the transpiration rates of an ocotillo plant near the laboratory above Tucson, Arizona. He reported that the leafless plant gave off only 13.7 milligrams of water in one hour. A few days later came his first desert rain, a real gully-washer. Two days after the rain, he was amazed to note that the ocotillo stems were covered with new leaves and were now tran-spiring 345 milligrams of water per hour. By five days after the rain, the transpiration rate was an astounding 1,876.6 milligrams per hour, *137 times* the rate before the rain! Within ten days however, the drought had set in again, the ocotillo had dropped its leaves and its transpiration rates returned to the earlier, near-quiescent level. It seems logical that desert plants would be water misers, but that isn't always true. Like ocotillo, many go absolutely wild after the infre-quent rains, squandering water as long as their roots can pull it from the soil. But when the soil dries out, these lavish spenders do what we humans can't seem to learn to do: live without until the next rain.

Between rains, ocotillo shuts its activities down to a barely per-ceptible level, respiring just enough to stay alive. Its tough stems are coated with a thick layer of waxes that retard evaporation and prevent harmful ultraviolet rays from damaging the delicate inner tissues. A green layer of cells just under the outer skin contains chlorophyll, enabling the leafless stems to produce enough food to keep the plant's metabolism barely ticking. And ocotillo is fiercely armored. When its leaves dry and fall off, the leaf stem splits longi-tudinally, leaving behind a pointed stub that dries into a hard thorn. Most grazers avoid ocotillo's spiny defenses, although deer browse the branch tips and peccaries are reported to tear the plant apart with their hoofs to get at the tender base.

Ocotillo's other miracle does not require rain. In the hottest, driest weeks of spring and early summer when other desert plants turn brown, ocotillo draws on its stored food and water and bursts into bloom. Its branch tips flame with dense spikes of fiery red, tubular blossoms, brilliant as flares. Hummingbirds, orioles, bees, wasps, and other nectar-feeders flock to drink from the inch-long, sweet flowers, and, flying from food source to food source, carry pollen to fertilize the blossoms. The Tohono O'odham of the Sonoran Desert once ate the sweet blossoms like candy. Tohono O'odham women also rubbed the reddish flower stalks on their cheeks for rouge. The Coahuilla of the Mojave Desert drank a sugary beverage made from ocotillo flowers.

Ocotillo's relatively long and tough stems make splendid building materials. Traditional Tohono O'odham houses are constructed of mud-plastered ocotillo limbs. The thorny stems are also thrust into the ground close together to form impenetrable fences and corrals. Sometimes the stems take root, forming living ocotillo barriers.

Ocotillo is the northernmost species of the Fouquieriaceae, a subtropical plant family comprised of less than a dozen species—all oddities. One of ocotillo's weirdest relatives was named by Godfrey Sykes, a colleague of my great-grandfather at the Desert Botanical Lab. According to the story, several lab scientists were on a survey trip in México when Sykes spotted a "forest" of bizarre trees that looked exactly like giant, upside-down albino carrots. The dimpled, swollen trunks of these strange trees stretch as tall as thirty feet, narrowing from three feet across at the base to just a few inches at the top. Their slender, spiny branches sprout randomly and grow whichever way, sometimes in circles. Looking through his telescope at the bizarre trees, Sykes exclaimed, "Ho, ho, a boojum, definitely a boojum!" The name—that of a mythical being native to far-off lands in Lewis Carroll's *The Hunting of the Snark*—stuck.

Whenever I look at the leafless, thorny clumps of ocotillo stalks studding desert hillsides, I am reminded of my great-grandfather and the insatiable curiosity that propelled him to the Sonoran Desert in 1903. I bless him for passing on not only his thirst for knowledge, but his sense of wonder as well.

COSTA'S HUMMINGBIRD

Colibri coronivioleta desértico
Calypte costae

> *If I were a female hummingbird perched still*
> *And quiet on an upper myrtle branch*
> *In the spring afternoon and if you were a male ...*
>
> *And if I watched how you fell, plummeting before me,*
> *And how you rose again and fell, with such mastery*
> *That I believed for a moment you were the sky....*
> —Pattiann Rogers, "The Hummingbird: A Seduction"

NAME: Costa's hummingbird is named for Louis Marie Pantaleon Costa, Marquis de Beau-Regard, a nineteenth-century French hummingbird collector. *Colibri* is an Indian word for "hummingbird"; *coroniviol*, "violet-crowned" in Spanish, refers to the male's iridescent purple head; *desértico* means "of the desert." *Calypte*, "covered" in Greek, is an obscure reference; *costae* is the Latinized version of Costa.

SIZE: Three inches long with wingspread of up to 4½ inches; weight about three grams, or equal to a penny

COLOR: Both sexes have bronze green upper parts and grayish white underparts; male sports an iridescent amethyst head, throat, and feathers that extend down the side of his face like sidewhiskers

RANGE: The Mojave and Sonoran Deserts north as far as southern Nevada and extreme southeastern Utah, plus coastal chaparral of Southern California and Baja California, México; occasionally east into the Chihuahuan Desert

HABITAT: Desert, arid shrubby foothills, chaparral

It is difficult to write about hummingbirds without lapsing into superlatives. When these tiny birds arrive in the deserts in late winter and early spring, darting through the air in blurs of brilliant color, squabbling in high-pitched voices over the best feeding sites, and performing their arcing display flights, it seems as if the air itself has burst into dazzling life.

Named for the sound of their hovering wings, hummingbirds were called "jewels of the air" by early naturalists for their sparkling, iridescent colors and astonishing aerial acrobatics. Hummingbirds are the only birds that can fly backwards, and one of the few birds that can truly hover, beating their wings to hang in place in still air. *Colibris* can also fly sideways and straight up and down. Huge flight muscles, comprising over a third of their body weight, pump their wings as fast as eighty times per second. Their stiff, broad tails act as rudders, facilitating lightning-fast midair turns, sudden feints, and fluid arcing dives.

To power their incredible flight and to maintain a constant body temperature, hummingbirds' metabolisms operate in hyperdrive. (With a large surface area relative to their mass, hummingbirds lose body heat quickly.) Their metabolic rates are the fastest of all warm-blooded creatures, except perhaps shrews. Thus, these tiny creatures eat voraciously, pumping nectar from flowers and feeders with the brushlike tip of their long tongue, and snatching insects and spiders off of plants or out of the air. But hummingbirds don't feed constantly. Instead, *colibris* make an average of fifteen foraging trips in an hour, each lasting less than a minute, and they perch for about four minutes between feedings. It seems that the average transit time for nectar through a hummingbird's gut is about one hour and they must rest to make space for more food.

On hot days, hummingbirds have to dissipate the tremendous heat generated by their metabolism and their hovering flight, or burn up. Like all birds, hummingbirds pant to keep cool, evaporating enormous amounts of water this way—a female Costa's hummingbird may lose nearly half of her body weight in water in one day. In order to rehydrate and fuel their metabolisms, hummingbirds must drink an amount of nectar equal to their body weight in water each day. If an adult human had the same energy and water needs, she'd have to eat 300 pounds of food a day and drink 150 gallons of water! At night, and on cool or rainy days hummingbirds lapse into torpor, a comalike state, to save energy—otherwise their ravenous metabolisms would quickly bankrupt their slender food stores. They lower their body temperature as much as 50 degrees and their metabolic rate to one-third of normal, in order to keep from starving to death.

Tiny creatures with high energy needs and a high potential for dehydration seem ill-suited to desert life. Indeed, many species of *colibris* avoid the desert, passing through only in migration, and those that reside there usually chose relatively verdant habitats near water or human-created oases. Costa's hummingbirds, however, exploit the most xeric, most extreme habitats the desert offers (hence *desértico* in their Spanish name). Costa's hummingbirds nest in the lower elevations of the Mojave and Sonoran Deserts, often in dry arroyos, arriving as early as February, when nighttime temperatures may still drop below freezing. By the time their young fledge, however, daytime temperatures often soar into the hundreds. By exploiting these difficult habitats, Costa's hummingbirds benefit from the lack of competition with other hummingbird species; but they take big risks, too, staking the success of their breeding season—and perhaps their lives—on food sources as ephemeral as the winter rains and conditions as harsh as any in the desert.

These tiny hummingbirds also migrate differently than other hummingbirds. Instead of the usual north-south movement, they seem to move laterally or altitudinally, from coastal and foothill environments into the deserts and back again in response to seasonal changes. (Their migration patterns are not clearly understood.) Costa's hummingbirds arrive in the deserts in late winter, and many are gone by early summer, returning again after the worst of the heat has passed in the fall. But where human habitat has modified the desert's seasonal food shortages, these *colibris* seem to be modifying their migration patterns. Where a year-round supply of nectar is available from flowers in yards and gardens, more Costa's hummingbirds remain all year.

Colibri's brilliant colors and awe-inspiring aerobatics are all for one purpose: reproduction. Male Costa's hummingbirds arrive in the nesting habitat earlier than females, and immediately establish territories consisting of stands of blossoming, nectar-bearing plants. They declare their space and attract mates by performing dazzling display flights. A male darts upward as high as 100 feet in the air, until he is just a tiny black speck against the blue sky, then literally screams earthward in an arcing dive, all the while making a shrill, high-pitched whining noise. At the bottom of the dive, he arcs upwards again, tracing a giant **U** in the air. Then he flies back to his starting point, and dives earthward over and over again, a purple and emerald blur of desire.

If a female is impressed, the two fly off together and mate. After their brief coupling, she builds a nest of small bits of bark and other plant materials, held together with cobwebs harvested from abandoned spider works and laced to a shrub or tree branch with thin bark strips. Once the thimble-shaped nest is complete, the female lays two eggs, two days apart. The eggs, each about the size of a navy bean, hatch in fifteen to eighteen days; the tiny hummingbirds, fed insects and spiders by their hard-working mother, are ready to leave the nest in about three weeks. The father, however, returns to his perch after mating, and resumes his heart-stopping aerial acrobatics, angling for other willing females. Hummingbird males are built for passing on the genes, not for housework.

If I were a female Costa's hummingbird, sitting still and quiet on a yucca leaf, and a male screamed earthward by me time and again, I'd be seduced by his dazzling display. Who could resist such a breathtaking demonstration of desire?

Big Sacaton

Zacatón
Sporobolus wrightii

> Encamped at sundown on the Jornada. No wood nor water; grass
> plenty. Cooked with the brush that lay around on the plain, sufficient for
> the purpose.
> —J. H. Byrne (1855) in EXPLORATIONS AND SURVEYS ...
> FROM THE MISSISSIPPI RIVER TO THE PACIFIC OCEAN,
> VOL. II

NAME: Sacaton comes from the Spanish, *zacate,* meaning "grass," "herb," or "hay." *Zacatón,* the Spanish name, is also from *zacate. Sporobolus* means "seed-thrower" in Greek, because the relatively large seeds drop readily to the ground; *wrightii* is for Charles Wright, who, as botanist to the first U.S.–Mexican Boundary Survey in the 1850s, collected and preserved some 2,500 plants.

SIZE: A robust bunchgrass growing up to six feet tall, the bunches sometimes three feet across; panicle (flower cluster) one to two feet tall and branching like a fish's skeleton, with curving "ribs" springing from a central "spine"

COLOR: Leaves and stalks pale green in summer, grayish the rest of the year

RANGE: From 2,000 to 7,000 feet elevation, western Texas to Southern California, south to central Mexico

HABITAT: Swales with sandy, alluvial soil, including riverbanks, washes, plains, and valley flats; much of its habitat has been disturbed by farming and grazing.

Obscure flowers and a bewildering array of characteristics discourage many people from becoming acquainted with grasses —they seem harder to identify than other plants. One native grass, big sacaton, stands out so distinctly, however—its coarse, gray green clumps growing to six feet tall —that it is easily recognized, even from a car zooming along a highway. Big sacaton is not as well known as saguaro cacti or Joshua trees, but, like those familiar desert characters, its presence marks a certain kind of desert. Where tall clumps of big sacaton crowd sandy swales, you can be pretty sure that—no matter what the surrounding landscape looks like now —it was once desert grassland, a unique plant community dominated by grasses adapted to thrive in the desert's searing heat and lengthy drought.

When most of us think of deserts, we don't think of grass. In fact, we usually equate *grass* with *green* and deserts are most definitely *not* lush, green landscapes. However, grasses once dominated large parts of the Chihuahuan, Sonoran, and Great Basin Deserts. Still, these were never verdant green expanses: grass plants covered no more than half the soil surface, and desert grasses spend half of the year dormant, bleached by the endless sun, and thus are not particularly green. Moreover, the deserts we see are shadows of their former selves, the grasses long removed by historic overgrazing and fire suppression, and contemporary groundwater mining and clearing for agriculture and development. We have forgotten that *desert* includes *grass*.

In fact, grasses were once so abundant that desert grasslands were the base of a thriving native hay industry. Between 1850 and 1920, says geographer Conrad Bahre, haying machines plying the Sonoran Desert grasslands of southern Arizona supplied the fodder for the scores of horses, burros, and mules in the region's cities, towns, mining camps, and military posts. In just the year 1899, says Bahre, Arizona farmers harvested 9,524 tons of wild hay, over half of that from the desert grasslands. (And that figure may underestimate the total. Native grass hay harvested by ranchers, Native Americans, and nonfarm entrepreneurs was not counted in the data.) In New Mexico, according to botanists E. O. Wooton and Paul C. Standly in a 1911 survey, "In certain places not far from Silver City [big sacaton] grows abundantly. . . . [I]t has been cut here and at other places in that region as hay grass. Liverymen prefer it . . . to alfalfa for buggy horses that are rented out for hard service." Today, it is hard to visualize hay machines and crews working the mesquite and creosote bush shrublands that grow where grasses once flourished.

Where did the grasses go? It is a familiar story in the West: enthusiastic overexploitation. After the Civil War, thousands of settlers, miners, and army folk—along with hundreds of thousands of their livestock—moved into the Southwest. Southeastern Arizona, home to some of the richest and most productive of the desert grasslands, boasted an estimated 377,000 cattle in 1891, along with several hundred thousand sheep. Photographs taken at the turn of the century of areas once covered with tough desert grasses show moonscapes grazed to bare dirt. The effects of overgrazing were exacerbated by suppression of natural fires, giving juniper, mesquite, sagebrush, creosote bush, cholla cactus, and other woody plants the advantage. Today, groundwater pumping for irrigated farming and urban use draws down water tables in many places, making the desert too dry to support perennial grasses.

Big sacaton and most other grasses of the hot deserts thrived for millennia by developing special adaptations to the searing heat and lengthy droughts. These so-called "warm-season grasses" sleep through the dry months of spring. They don't green up and grow until the summer sun heats the soil. But their preference is less about temperature than water. Half or more of their yearly precipitation comes in summer. Many of these grasses have also evolved an alternate kind of photosynthesis, the process by which plants convert carbon dioxide and sunlight into sugars for food, and, in so doing, release the oxygen we humans breathe. Instead of opening their pores in the daytime to take in carbon dioxide and give off oxygen as plants conventionally do, big sacaton and others do their gas exchange during the cooler and moister nighttime. This alternate process is less efficient at converting sunlight to food, but more efficient at conserving water. Sunlight is abundant in the desert; water is not.

When I see the tall, coarse, grayish green clumps of big sacaton crowding a swale in the desert, or notice the fish-spine tracery of their sere flower stalks against the winter-blue sky, my heart sings. Green or no green, *zacatón* says "beauty" to me. Its presence says that the groundwater tables are high and that the surrounding grasslands are healthy, more like *grass*lands and less like *shrub*lands. It says that Cassin's or other grassland sparrows are likely trilling their thin songs nearby, that moonlight-colored kit foxes are hunting the area at night, that desert pronghorn graze the neighborhood, and that, in rainy years, wildflowers will bloom in starry abundance. The sight of a swale of big sacaton says that all is well with at least one small part of the world.

GIANT DESERT HAIRY SCORPION

Escorpión
Hadrurus arizonensis

> *For a real glimpse into an almost vanished world, one should look ...*
> *at a scorpion who so obviously has no business lingering into the twen-*
> *tieth century.*
> —Joseph Wood Krutch, THE DESERT YEAR

NAME: Giant desert hairy scorpions are the largest in the deserts, and are covered with erect dark brown hairs. *Escorpión* is "scorpion" in Spanish. *Hadrurus* comes from the Greek root for "stout," apparently referring to the scorpion's size; *arizonensis* means "of Arizona."

SIZE: Adults grow to 5½ inches long

COLOR: Cephalothorax (the scorpion's head) black, edged with yellow; the rest of the body pale yellow; the young lack pigment until their first molt

RANGE: Found throughout the hot deserts of the southwestern states and northern México

HABITAT: In the daytime, under stones or in crevices; at night, hunting on the ground in shrub deserts and grasslands

On dark nights late in the summer, Scorpius the scorpion rises near the southern horizon in the southwestern United States and northern México, with her tail of stars curled over her back, and the bright orange star Anatares marking her pincers.

Scorpius is a very aptly named constellation: scorpions are nocturnal, and are most active on warm summer nights. Although they look like miniature, terrestrial lobsters—complete with a long, segmented tail and lobsterlike, enlarged front legs—scorpions are arachnids, related to spiders. Like their spider cousins, scorpions sport multiple pairs of eyes, but, unlike spiders, scorpions hunt exclusively by feel. They detect the vibrations of approaching animals with special sensory organs under the cuticles on their legs and attached to hairs on their feet. Biologists speculate that by differentiating between the times that the vibrations reach the different organs, scorpions can ascertain the exact location of potential prey. A scorpion can precisely locate prey as far away as four inches in total darkness.

Once a scorpion locates a potential meal, it grabs the prey with its pincerlike pedipalps—front legs—and immobilizes it with a swift downward thrust of its abdomen, embedding its stinger in the victim's body. As the *escorpión* contracts its tail muscles for the downward thrust, the muscles squeeze two venom glands at the base of the stinger, pushing venom through the hollow, hypodermic-needle-like tip.

Scorpion venom varies in its toxicity: in healthy adult humans its effects are usually no worse than a bad bee sting. In extreme cases, however, it can cause staggering gait, drooling, convulsions, respiratory paralysis, and even heart failure. Ironically, the North American scorpion possessing the most toxic venom is also the smallest species, the two-inch-long bark scorpion; the venom of the giant desert hairy scorpion is comparatively mild.

Scorpions are not picky about their food. They will snatch anything that they can subdue, including spiders and insects, small lizards and snakes, and other scorpions—even members of their own species. Such cannibalism has distinct advantages, writes evolutionary biologist John Alcock in his book, *Sonoran Desert Summer.* Not only are small scorpions easy and relatively safe prey because their tiny stingers can inject very little venom, but the tissues of a member of one's own species provide the perfect diet. No wonder then, that cannibalism is a fairly common practice; fish, frogs, toads, protozoans, rotifers, ground squirrels, spiders, preying mantids, centipedes, and robberflies also indulge. According to Alcock, eating your fellows may enhance your chances of passing on your own genes. For example, mosquitofish fed a diet of their fellows grew larger or developed larger gonads, both advantageous for reproductive success. Of course, a cannibal interested in the success of her own genes must be careful to eat only unrelated individuals, not her own kin!

Courtship among cannibalistic creatures is—naturally—a delicate matter. A male scorpion clasps his intended by her pincers, holding fast while he leads her in a "dance," moving backwards, sideways, or around in circles until he maneuvers her over a suitable surface where he can deposit his bag of sperm and she can suck it into her genital opening. A few months or a year later (depending on the species), she bears dozens of baby scorpions. Looking just like miniatures of their parents—except that they are colorless—the little ones climb aboard their mother's back and ride there, sheltered by her formidable stinger, until after their first molt. Such solicitous maternal care makes sense in a society where elders often eat youngsters.

Scorpions are elegantly adapted to survive desert climates. By hunting only at night, they avoid the hottest, driest weather entirely. During the day and during prolonged dry spells, they take refuge in burrows, under rocks, or in any spot that remains cooler and moister than the desert surface (including in air-conditioned buildings). Their exoskeleton, comprised of several layers of wax, forms such an efficient barrier to evaporation that they lose water at rates lower than that of any other creature. Still, should scorpions become dehydrated, they can survive losing 40 percent of their body weight in water. (We humans, by comparison, are in bad shape after losing just 10 percent of our body weight to dehydration.) Scorpions can also survive body temperatures that would cook humans and most other desert arthropods, up to 113 degrees.

Scorpions look like ancient life forms, and indeed, they have been around a long time. Fossils of scorpions date to back before there was much other sign of terrestrial life, long before spiders or insects evolved. An antediluvian relative of scorpions—literally "from before the flood"—often gets confused with its venomous relative, but is actually harmless to humans. Giant vinegarones or whip scorpions look fearsome, with a black, flattened body, a tiny head sporting multiple pairs of eyes, a ferocious-looking pair of clublike, inward-curving pincers, and a several-inch-long, whiplike tail; and they grow to six inches long, longer than giant desert hairy scorpions. Despite their appearance, however, giant vinegarones are armed only with a vinegarlike spray. Its pungent odor inspires their curious common name. Nocturnal like true scorpions, vinegarones feel their way in darkness with a pair of long, slender front legs that continuously sweep the ground in front of their body like antennae.

According to the ancient Greeks, Scorpius the scorpion terrified the horses of the sun while they were being driven by Phaeton, the young son of Helios, the sun god. Phaeton lost control of the frightened steeds and they plunged earthwards, searing a long streak of the earth before they were stopped by Zeus. Fittingly, scorpions now inhabit the deserts created by their mythical starry ancestor.

SCREWBEAN MESQUITE

Tornillo
Prosopis pubescens

> *The mesquite is God's best thought in all this desertness.*
> —Mary Austin, THE LAND OF LITTLE RAIN

NAME: Mesquite comes from the Spanish *mezquite,* a corruption of *mizquitl,* the Aztec word for these small, thorny, arid-country trees. *Tornillo,* "little screw" in Spanish, describes the tightly coiled, corkscrew-shaped pods. *Prosopis* is a Greek word for "burdock," a spiny herb; *pubescens* refers to downy hairs on the leaflets.

SIZE: A small tree up to thirty feet high; the trunk to three feet around

COLOR: Bark pale gray; flowers yellow and catkinlike; leaves pale green and divided into eight or more leaflets

RANGE: Below 4,000 feet elevation from southwest Texas to Southern California, south into northern México, north as far as southern Nevada and southwestern Utah

HABITAT: Grows in the *bosque,* or riparian woodland, along arroyos, desert rivers and streams, and around waterholes.

Long, long ago, begins a story in the *Diccionario de Aztequismos,* before the Europeans reached America, Quetzalcoatl, god of the wind and rain, appeared in human form. He taught the Mexican people many things: to build houses of stone, to weave garments, to make pottery, and to do feather work. For these things, says the story, Quetzalcoatl was highly honored. But when he attempted to do away with human sacrifice, the priests opposed him. Quetzalcoatl grew angry. In his displeasure, he made the land arid, metamorphosing its cacao trees into *mizquitl,* mesquite. Then Quetzalcoatl disappeared over the western sea to return no more.

Several species of mesquite, small spreading trees or large shrubs with edible, beanlike pods and stout thorns, grow throughout the hot desert regions of the Americas. In the Southwest, these thorny trees owe their present ubiquity to the domestic cow, not the god Quetzalcoatl. Once confined to arroyo bottoms and desert floodplains, where they formed dense *bosques* or woodlands, mesquites were seeded throughout the uplands by the enormous herds of cattle brought to the southern Southwest and northern México in the

1800s. Cows relish the sugary, bean-shaped pods of mesquite trees. The stony seeds, however, pass right through their digestive systems, the tough seed cover thinned by the process and the seed thus ready to germinate. As the increasing cows grazed the dense cover of grass from the desert grasslands, they planted mesquite seeds, in millions of pats of fertilizer—cow pies. Without grass and other fine fuels to burn, natural fires, which once may have kept mesquites under control by killing the abundant seedlings, decreased. At the same time, billions of prairie dogs, which eat mesquite seedlings by the score, were poisoned almost to extinction by predator control programs. As a result, mesquite now dominates more than 130,000 square miles of the southwestern United States and northern México—an area equal to half the size of the state of Texas.

While the two dominant species of mesquite benefited from cattle grazing, the desert's other mesquite species actually has grown scarcer. Screwbean mesquite or *tornillo*—named for the tight, spiral curl of its seed pods—is the least common, but most distinctive, of the mesquites. This graceful tree with the corkscrew pods is a riparian species. It once dominated the extensive deciduous woodlands that filled valley bottoms along the floodplains of desert rivers and streams. Unfortunately for *tornillo*, its floodplain habitat is also most desirable for farming, grazing, and development. Over 90 percent of the Southwest's once-verdant, tangled *bosques* have been cleared, plowed, or dried up from stream channelization or groundwater over-pumping during the past century.

Like all mesquites, screwbean mesquite is a small, thorny tree with compound leaves. Desert plants tend to have small leaves—if they have leaves at all—in order to reduce heat gain from the glaring sun and to minimize evaporation of precious water. *Tornillo's* tiny leaflets—they are less than three-quarters of an inch long—are arranged along a stubby, two- to three-inch-long leaf stalk. From May to September, the tree's lacy canopy is dotted with fuzzy yellow flowers shaped like willow catkins.

Although the Aztecs may have thought mesquites a curse of the god Quetzalcoatl, scientists are now discovering that the thorny trees are actually a blessing to desert ecosystems and to desert-dwelling humans. Mesquites fertilize desert soils and provide food and homes for hundreds of kinds of desert animals. The hardy trees have a cooperative relationship with cyanobacteria, microscopic organisms that change nitrogen—a nutrient vital to plant growth—into a form accessible to plants. When mesquite sheds its tiny leaflets, the nitrogen-rich litter fertilizes eroded, nutrient-poor desert soils. Mesquite's clusters of fragrant flowers feed nectar-eaters from hummingbirds and beetles to honeybees. Mesquite honey is prized by humans for its delicate flavor. The tree canopy is home for all manner of species of insects, birds, and animals. And mesquite seed pods, rich in sugars, fiber, and minerals, sustain many desert lives, from borer beetles to javelina and humans.

People once depended on mesquite pods the way that we now depend on wheat. The pods were harvested in summer and stored in huge, tightly woven granary baskets as tall as an adult person. Ground in stone mortars or *metates*, dried mesquite pods yield a coarse, sweet meal called *pinole* in Spanish. (The stonelike seeds, however, are discarded. They are tooth-breakers!) Cooked with hot water, mesquite meal produces a sweet cereal, or a nutritious hot drink. Swirled with cold water, it is a delicious Instant Breakfast–like drink. Pinole is used in thin, crepelike doughs, tortillalike flatbreads, or dense, biscuitlike cakes. Fermented, pinole produces an intoxicating drink. Mesquite pods once furnished more than basic nutrition. As processed foods replaced mesquite and other desert foods for desert-dwelling Indians, the incidence of diabetes rose as well, eventually reaching today's epidemic levels. Health-care professionals and others have recently discovered the connection. Pinole, it seems, is perfect for a diabetes-preventing diet: it is rich in natural sugars and fiber, as well as calcium, magnesium, potassium, iron, and zinc, and helps stabilize blood sugar. *Los antepasados*—the old ones—are surely shaking their heads as we rediscover what they knew all along.

A young *tornillo* grows in my backyard, planted in honor of the *bosque* that grew where my subdivision now sprawls. Just a little slip of a gray stem five years ago, its three graceful trunks now stretch fifteen feet upwards. In summer, its pale green canopy hums with the buzzing of hummingbird and bee wings; in winter, its bare branches etch a delicate tracery against the clear blue sky, a reminder of the changes this landscape has endured.

WESTERN DIAMONDBACK
RATTLESNAKE

Vibora de cascabel
Croatulus atrox

> *Where I was raised, rattlesnakes are a threat, and you kill them when you see them. . . . There is also little hysteria about snakes. You watch for them; if you see one, you kill it. . . . I come from snake-killing people.*
> —Teresa Jordan, RIDING THE WHITE HORSE HOME

NAME: Named for the diamond-shaped markings on its back. *Vibora de cascabel,* "viper of the small bell" in Spanish, refers to the snake's rattle. *Croatulus* comes from the Greek root for "rattle" or "castanet"; *atrox* is Latin for "hideous," "terrible," or "cruel."

SIZE: Adults grow as long as seven feet, with a body as large around as a man's forearm. This is the largest western rattlesnake.

COLOR: Varies with habitat, from gray and brown to pinkish, yellowish, or even black, with light brown to black diamond-shaped blotches on its back, but faded overall, as if dusty. Also called "coontail" for the broad black and white bands on its tail.

RANGE: Sea level to around 7,000 feet elevation; from southeastern California east to Arkansas and east Texas; south into central México.

HABITAT: Dry, sandy, or rocky habitats from deserts uphill onto the mountains

NOTES: This is the most aggressive western rattlesnake; it will stand its ground when threatened. It can live as long as twenty-six years.

The biggest rattlesnake that I've ever seen was also the first one that I remember. Early one summer morning of my childhood, my brother and I were out exploring around our desert campground. Under a soaring sandstone overhang, we nearly stumbled over a huge western diamondback rattler, a grandmother of snakes, sunning herself on a patch of bare rock. Her heavy body was bigger around than our arms and looked to our astonished eyes to be much longer than we were tall.

Rattlesnakes are a fact of life in the hot deserts. Eleven species live in northern México and the United States' Southwest, more than in any other region of the Americas. Resident *cascabeles* range in size from the diminutive, foot-long twin-spotted rattlesnake to the western diamondback.

Rattlesnakes get their name from their rattles, loosely interlocking horny segments ending their tail. They acquire a new rattle segment each time they shed their skin—up to four times per year depending on how healthy and well fed they are, and their age (young rattlers grow faster and thus shed more often). Their Spanish name, *cascabel*, "little bell," alludes to one of the sounds made as the loose segments vibrate against each other. Depending on the rattler's size, its level of agitation, and the number of rattle segments, the rattle can sound like dry leaves crackling, a cicada's slow clicking, a burst of steam, or the clattering of castanets. A rattler's buzzing warning and coiled stance is a defensive measure evolved because these large, heavy-bodied snakes cannot race away swiftly. Hence the clear message: "Back off!"

Many people fear rattlers, and no wonder. One bite of a rattle-snake's specialized fangs, and you are history—if you are a mouse, rat, or other small animal. The potent poisons in rattler's neurotoxic venom interfere with the nervous systems of their victims, causing convulsions, paralysis, and death. Although rattlesnake bites have serious consequences for humans, the likelihood of being killed in the Southwest by a venomous animal like a *cascabel* is slim: you are twenty times more likely to be struck by lightning and 300 times more likely to be murdered by a fellow human being, writes evolutionary biologist James Alcock. Rattlesnakes, he says, developed their sophisticated poisons for hunting and defense, not to kill humans. If you stay out of their way, they will stay out of yours.

Cascabeles are master hunters. Western diamondbacks, like most rattlesnakes, do the majority of their stalking from evening until early morning, avoiding the hottest hours of the day. They slither along the ground, flicking their sensitive forked tongues to pick up the smell and airborne vibrations of potential meals. They can accurately pinpoint the location of prey by detecting its body heat with their loreal pits, specialized sensory organs on either side of their head behind their nostrils. So acute are loreal pits that a rattler hunting in total darkness can "see" a mouse from up to a foot away by detecting its body heat.

Once a western diamondback is close to its prey, the snake strikes quickly, thrusting its powerful body forward and dispatching the animal with a sophisticated venom-dispensing mechanism. As a rattler bites, hollow fangs at the front of the its upper jaw swing down and forward, locking into place. The fangs stab the victim's flesh and drip venom into the wound in a single, swift thrust. Then the snake backs away, and waits for the venom to quell the animal's struggling. When its prey is quiet, the *cascabel* slithers forward and opens its mouth wider than seems possible, and swallows its meal whole, beginning at the head. With articulated jaws that open to nearly 180 degrees and flexible ribs, a rattler can swallow prey many times larger than its own diameter. Rattlers may ingest 40 percent of their body weight in a single meal, then crawl off to a sheltered place to sleep off their feast. Gluttony, however, can be fatal. Rattlesnake literature abounds with stories of overly ambitious snakes that tried to swallow prey too big and starved to death with their meal stuck in their gaping jaws.

Western diamondbacks hunt and eat a wide variety of prey — mostly rodents such as mice and kangaroo rats, but also rabbits, squirrels, birds, and lizards. By consuming rodents, these big snakes help maintain the balance between grazers and grazed. Without *cascabeles* and coyotes and the other rodent and rabbit predators, populations of these voracious grazers would quickly multiply —the old saw about breeding like a rabbit is based on fact —and soon the deserts would indeed be bare, lifeless places, the plants nibbled down to nothing.

Western diamondbacks are not often seen, partly because they are nocturnal, partly because they are elegantly camouflaged, the color of their background scales matching the overall color of the earth. Where rust red and orange sandstones weather to pinkish soil, for instance, they take on a pink hue. Or they acquire yellowish, gray, and tan or brown backgrounds, depending upon where they live. Western diamondbacks evolve their "local color" quickly in an evolutionary sense: on a two-thousand-year-old black basalt flow in southern New Mexico, these *cascabeles* are—you guessed it!—blackish.

Western diamondbacks den up in cold weather, hibernating in burrows in the ground or in spaces between rocks. On cool mornings in fall and early spring, they sun near their dens. Sometime during the summer, depending on the timing of the rains, they mate, twining together in sinuous, hours-long copulation. The pregnant female carries the developing eggs for several weeks. They hatch inside her: two to two dozen fully formed baby rattlers spill out and head off on their own. The young *cascabeles* are miniatures of their parents, except that they are born silent, with only one rattle segment.

Some people kill rattlesnakes whenever they see them. Fear, I can understand; thoughtless killing, I can't. In *Riding the White Horse Home*, Teresa Jordan tells of encountering a rattlesnake while hiking in the desert with friends. Without thinking, Jordan picks up a handful of stones and kills the snake. Her friends are horrified. Jordan examines her automatic reaction. She comes, she says, "from snake-killing people." Killing rattlers on the ranch where she grew up was a practical matter. But, Jordan admits after much thought, it didn't make sense to kill the snake there in the open desert. "Will I kill another snake?" she asks herself. "Not thoughtlessly," she decides. Still, Jordan acknowledges, changing her habitual antipathy towards rattlers is another question indeed.

I come from a snake-respecting people. I watch for rattlesnakes, and, well aware of their deadly potential, never hear their dry rattle without feeling a clutch of fear. But I leave them alone, believing in their right to share these arid landscapes. In "The Snake People," from her book *Dwellings*, Linda Hogan writes: "They have been here inhabiting the same dens for tens of thousands of generations, threading between rocks, stretching in the sun, disappearing into the grass. They belong here."

I don't remember now how long my brother and I stood, barely breathing, those years ago, our eyes fixed on the big rattler. But I can still picture clearly the heavy, diamond-patterned length of her body and the graceful wedge of her head. Even then, I was as aware of her beauty as I was of her venom. Eventually, we headed back to our campsite for breakfast, leaving the *cascabel* to sun. We knew, even then, that she belonged there, just as we did.

ARIZONA SISTER

Mariposa
Adelpha bredowii eulalia

> Most people are simply not aware of anything smaller than a robin;
> their senses are not adjusted to take in small wonders.... As Vladimir
> Nabokov observed in his memoirs, "It is astonishing how few people notice
> butterflies." Yet those who miss butterflies miss one of the greatest specta-
> cles of all, in sheer wonder and beauty if not in size.
>
> —Robert Michael Pyle, HANDBOOK FOR BUTTERFLY
> WATCHERS

N A M E : The dark upper wings are reminiscent of the coloring of a nun's habit, hence "sister"; Arizona is where this butterfly was described. *Mariposa* means "butterfly" in Spanish. *Adelpha* means "brother" in Greek, perhaps also a reference to the habitlike coloring; *bredowii* honors an entomologist named Bredow; *eulalia* is an obscure reference.
S I Z E : The butterfly's wingspan is 2⅞ to 3⅜ inches; the caterpillar is 1¼ inches long
C O L O R : Blackish brown above with a striking white band running diagonally across the upper wings and an orange patch at the tip of the upper forewing; below, the butterfly's wings are silvery with pale blue, white, brown, and orange marbling. The caterpillar is dark green above and olive brown below, colored like an oak leaf.
R A N G E : Southern Texas west to southern Arizona, north to central Utah, and south into México along the Sierra Madre
H A B I T A T : Oak woodlands and mountain canyons
N O T E S : A subspecies of the more widespread California sister.

As we rounded a blind corner in the steep dirt road, I shifted down and eased the car gently over a large rock. Cool air blew in the open windows. The leafy canopies of the oaks cast welcome patches of shade; a puddle spanned the road ahead. At the car's approach, the puddle seemed to fly off, taking to the air on bold black and white wings. I braked quickly. The illusion dissolved into large butterflies, dozens of them, fluttering above the road. "Look!" I exclaimed to my parents, my companions on this trip into the Huachuca Mountains near Tucson. We watched as the cloud of butterflies settled to earth to drink at the puddle again, admiring their silvery underwings and white-striped, dark upper wings tipped with orange spots.

The deserts are studded with mountain ranges, like so many islands rising from expanses of arid "sea." Like islands in the ocean, these mountain ranges offer worlds radically different from the surrounding seas—cooler and moister worlds, in this case, generally more hospitable to life. The taller ranges support broad bands of shady forest; even the small, sparsely clad mountains hide cool, green oases tucked deep in rocky canyons. Such mountain islands act as refugia, offering homes for species like black bears or thick-billed parrots that cannot survive in the hot, arid desert. Whether a golden grove of aspens in the mountains of the Great Basin Desert or a shimmering flock of *mariposas* such as the Arizona sisters that we startled that summer day in the Sonoran Desert's Huachucas, mountain islands harbor surprises for eyes accustomed to the sparse expanses of desert.

Arizona sisters live in oak woodlands, inhabiting the islands that ride high above the open seas of desert. Like all butterflies and moths, and many other insects, their lives are split into two radically different phases: a terrestrial, crawling phase and an airborne, winged phase. Our nomenclature for these phases reveals an interesting bias that has no basis in these creatures' biology: the terrestrial phase is called the "juvenile"; the winged phase, the "adult." As evolutionary biologist Stephen Jay Gould points out in an essay in *Natural History* magazine, the phases have no relationship to relative maturity. The two are simply different: the terrestrial creature's job is to eat and grow, the winged creature's, to reproduce. Only viewed in terms of human lives, writes Gould, would we label one phase "juvenile" and the other "adult." Those labels, he maintains, obscure the functions of the divergent parts of insects' lives, rather than illuminating them.

Arizona sisters' winged phase appears as early as April and as late as December, the delicate butterfly emerging from a chrysalis colored and shaped like an oak leaf. Once airborne, their main object is a basic one: to find a mate or mates. These eye-catching butterflies do feed—some species don't feed in their winged phase—but they spend most of the *mariposa* portion of their lives searching for a mate. Males patrol gulches and stream canyons in the oak woodlands with their peculiar flap-and-glide flight, on the hunt for females. Once a male spies a potential partner, he pursues her—over hill and dale if necessary—until she slows long enough for him to convince her to attach the end of her abdomen to his. Several days after mating, females search out oak trees and lay round, green eggs singly on the leaf edges. The tiny eggs look like small growths of leaf tissue.

The peculiar-looking caterpillars that hatch in several weeks go immediately to work. Their job: to eat and grow. Arizona sister caterpillars' humpbacked, two-tone green bodies sprout six fleshy tubercles—projections—from their back. Their oak-leaf-like color and generally knobby appearance may serve to disguise these fleshy, edible caterpillars from hungry predators like birds: motionless, an Arizona sister caterpillar looks quite unappetizing, like a green bird dropping. The larvae of most butterflies are picky eaters, and Arizona sisters are no exception. These green, bumpy caterpillars only consume the foliage of certain oak species, including Emory oak and Arizona white oak. Although picky, Arizona sister caterpillars have large appetites: they gobble enormous quantities of their chosen food.

Late-hatching Arizona sister caterpillars spend their first winter hibernating in the larval stage. After growing to full size the following spring, the larvae spin a two-horned, pale brown chrysalis around themselves. Inside this chrysalis, which looks just like a dead, in-rolled oak leaf suspended innocuously from an oak twig, their bodies undergo the magical metamorphosis from stout, lumpy, terrestrial caterpillars to satin-winged, graceful *mariposas.*

Fluttering and gliding through the shade of the oaks, Arizona sister butterflies seem like mirages, denizens of a cooler, moister world that might simply dissolve on a hot day. Indeed, when viewed from the desert below, the mountains and mesas where they live seem unbelievable, like the shimmering hallucinations of a feverish mind. Just like the *mariposas* that they harbor, however, these cool islands are real, and an integral part of the deserts' contradictory magic.

KIT FOX

Zorra de las praderas
Vulpes macrotis

> Like a shadowy something, it seemed to float ghostlike before us, then fade into the half-darkness before coming alongside or following behind. So careful was it not to come too near, so close was its color to that of the silver sand, so silent was it of foot, that although we strained our eyes and ears we could not fully make out its outline or decide upon its true nature.
>
> —Edmund C. Jaeger, DESERT WILDLIFE

NAME: Kit fox refers to the small size and catlike grace of this fox. *Zorra de las praderas*, "fox of the meadows" in Spanish, is a misnomer since these foxes are consummate desert-dwellers. *Vulpes* is Latin for "fox"; *macrotis* means "big ears" in Greek.

SIZE: Up to thirty inches long, of which fully a foot is tail; adults weigh up to five pounds and stand just a foot tall at the shoulder

COLOR: Yellowish gray above, buff flanks and underparts, white throat and belly, black-tipped tail

RANGE: Lower elevations of the deserts and adjacent arid country of western New Mexico, Arizona, Nevada, and California, north to eastern Oregon and southern Idaho

HABITAT: Shrub deserts, grasslands, sand dunes, and alluvial plains

NOTES: The smallest wild canid in North America. Kit foxes can live ten years in captivity.

A day in the life of a kit fox begins at night. Waking from its slumber just as the evening shadows merge into darkness, a kit fox peers out of its burrow cautiously. Its oversized, furry ears swivel, listening attentively, its black eyes, seemingly large for its fist-sized head, are alert. If the coast is clear, the *zorrita*—small fox—emerges, stretches, then sets off on its nighttime rounds.

Kit foxes are shadowy hunters of the desert nights, silent as the owls that fly overhead. Camouflaged even on moonlit nights by fur as pale as the desert ground, *zorritas* hunt on feet silenced by the thick cushioning of hair between their toe pads. Their furry feet also give them good traction on loose, sandy desert soils and may insulate their skin from the often-hot ground. Kit foxes trot through the darkness, their oversized ears alert and functioning like parabolic reflectors to pick up and magnify even the slightest sound. Their large eyes gather what little light is available, and their keen noses can detect the smallest thread of scent. Still, hunting at night is a difficult way to make a living.

Biologists think that kit foxes probably chose a nocturnal life to avoid the desert's extreme heat and aridity. Being active only in the cooler, moister night and spending the day in a climate-controlled subterranean burrow allows these small foxes to save water and energy, and thus to have a better chance of survival. Hunting only at night also allows kit foxes to avoid becoming dinner for larger predators, since fewer large predators are nocturnal. There is one significant trade-off to their nocturnal habits: hunting at night sometimes puts kit foxes in competition with coyotes for the same food. Coyotes do kill *zorritas*, possibly because of such competition.

In order to increase their success at finding food, kit foxes specialize, mainly hunting one kind of prey: the kangaroo rat, a foot-long, common desert rodent named for its upright, hopping gait, enlarged hind legs, and long, furry tail. A full-grown kit fox needs about six ounces of meat per night to survive. That's one large kangaroo rat or two smaller ones, depending on the species. So intimately intertwined are the lives of the small foxes and the rodents with the peculiar hopping gait that kit foxes live only where kangaroo rats do: a map outlining the range of the eight subspecies of kit fox closely matches a map showing the distribution of kangaroo rats. Both thrive in the driest parts of the deserts because neither needs to drink water. Kangaroo rats metabolize all the water that they need from the seeds they eat; kit foxes get their water from the flesh of their rodent prey.

Kangaroo rats live alone in underground burrows topped with a distinctive mound of earth and accessed through several entrances. A hunting kit fox searches for a kangaroo rat mound, then stops to listen for the occupant. With relatively short legs, the *zorrita* isn't adapted to coyotelike chases requiring great stamina or speed. Instead, the kit fox uses its keen hearing and digs for its dinner, the earth flying. If it is lucky and skilled, the fox snatches the kangaroo rat from its burrow before it can escape. Kit foxes also stalk their nocturnal prey out in the open, crouching catlike and creeping forward with silent grace, until they are close enough to pounce, stiff-legged, for the kill. When kangaroo rats are not plentiful, kit foxes hunt other rodents, jackrabbits, insects, and young desert tortoises and Gila monsters.

Whether the night's hunt was successful or not, a kit fox returns to its den before dawn lights the sky. Kit foxes are the only wild canids to use dens year-round; dens protect these diminutive foxes both from the adverse climate and from larger predators. Kit foxes spend about half the year alone, in their own den. In winter, male and female *zorritas* pair up, mate, and begin preparing a different den—used year after year—for the coming family. They haul out last year's debris and dig new entrances. In February or March, four or five pups are born. For the first month of their life, the mother nurses the pups; the father hunts for food. Later, both parents hunt. Kit fox families stay together until autumn, when the pups are full-grown and ready to live on their own.

Along with coyotes, kit foxes play an important part in controlling desert rodent populations. For example, parent kit foxes must bring the pups about 100 pounds of meat during the two months they feed them—the equivalent of about 600 kangaroo rats! Yet people have harassed these little foxes almost into extinction: *zorritas* are trapped, shot, poisoned, and their habitat destroyed by farming or suburban growth. Once common throughout the West—if not often seen because of their nocturnal existence—kit foxes are now endangered in some parts of their range.

Driving home one morning, I spotted a small, buff-colored animal with large, pointed ears lying dead on the highway. My husband stopped the car and I walked back to see what it was. Its diminutive size, moonlight-colored fur, large, pointed ears, delicate doglike face, and short legs were distinctive: a *zorrita*. I carefully picked up the fox's limp body, carried it off the pavement, and laid it in the shade of a desert shrub. As I walked away, I realized sadly that I'd seen only one wild kit fox since I moved to the desert: the dead one that I had just laid down.

TUBE-FORMING TERMITE

Hormiga blanca
Gnathamitermes tubiformans

> *Descended from cockroach-like ancestors as far back as 150 million years ago, early in the Mesozoic Era, these curious insects have converged in evolution toward ants in superficial appearance and social behavior, but they have nothing else in common.*
> —Bert Hölldobler and Edward O. Wilson, JOURNEY TO THE ANTS

NAME: Tube-forming termites are named for the distinctive mud tubes that they build for shelter while they consume woody material above ground. *Hormiga blanca,* or "white ant," in Spanish, refers to the termites' color and the misconception that these small, colonial creatures are ants. *Gnathamitermes* means "jawed wood-worm" in Latin; *tubiformans,* "tube-forming," also refers to the mud tubes.

SIZE: From one-quarter to five-eighths inches long, depending on the caste

COLOR: Their soft bodies are white or yellowish; the reproductives are black with clear, net-veined wings

RANGE: The Chihuahuan Desert of northern México, southern New Mexico, and southwest Texas; other species of tube-forming termites inhabit the other deserts

HABITAT: Wherever soils are suitable for excavating their extensive underground homes

NOTES: These termites are most active after warm-season rains. Termites and ants are by far the most abundant insects in the deserts.

T ermites and ants act as the earthworms of the deserts. Although small in size, these insects are prodigiously abundant —hundreds of them may occupy each square yard of soil, and their collective impact is profound. Without the earth-churning and fertilizing activities of termites and ants, desert soils would absorb less water and eventually cease to be fertile. Plants would no longer be able to grow, and animal life would thus starve.

Termites and ants seem similar: both are social insects. Both live in underground nests, in colonies consisting of several generations of sterile, wingless workers and soldiers whose functions are to nurture and protect their siblings. Like ant colonies, termite colonies are considered superorganisms, groups of lives that act in concert, as if they were parts of some larger being. Termites and ants both produce winged generations that fly from the colony to mate and found new colonies. With so many similarities, it is no wonder that termites are often called *hormigas blancas*—white ants.

In reality, however, the two kinds of insects are very different. Unlike ants' old girls' clubs, termite colonies contain both females *and* males. An ant queen spawns a new colony alone; termite queens found their colonies with the help of their mates. Termites are recyclers, and only eat woody plant material. Ants, on the other hand, play many different roles and eat a wide variety of foods. Although both ant and termite colonies are differentiated into separate castes, or roles, ants are born with a fixed role in life—worker, soldier, or reproductive. In termite colonies, however, individuals may change castes—a worker may grow the enormous jaws of a soldier, for instance—in response to chemical signals from the colony. Termites and ants are not even related: termites probably developed from cockroaches. The similarities between ants and termites stem from convergent evolution, two very different types of creatures making similar adaptive choices in response to similar living conditions.

Like all termites, tube-forming termites spend most of their lives in their extensive nests, which for tube-forming termites are underground, comprised of many-foot-long tunnels and galleries stretching deep into the soil. Hatched from eggs laid by the colony's reigning queen, individual termites may grow into workers, soldiers, or reproductives. Workers feed and groom the colony's young and queen and king, maintain the nest, and forage for food above ground. Soldiers protect the colony with their strong jaws or with chemical defenses, depending on the species. Reproductives are the winged, fertile generation that flies from the nest to mate and found new colonies. The role of each individual termite at any given time is dependent on the colony's specific needs.

Termites, like many insects, communicate with chemical signals. Termites' chemical "vocabulary" is diverse and sophisticated, ranging from alarm signals exuded in response to distress, to trails laid to point the way to food, to hormones which cause individuals to change castes. These social insects can identify members of their own colony by specific chemical "badges." Soldiers defending the nest eject or kill intruders whose badges do not match. One termite predator, the assassin bug, cleverly circumvents this identification system by disguising itself with the carcasses of dead termites. Under its correct-smelling camouflage, an assassin bug wanders a termite colony unrecognized—like the proverbial wolf in sheep's clothing—eating its fill.

Besides "talking" with chemicals, termites also use chemicals for defense. Species of termites that forage in the open equip their soldier castes with chemical weaponry including irritants, contact poisons, toxicants, and glues. One species has even evolved a squirt gun–like nozzle on the heads of its soldiers. These termites can aim the nozzle and eject a clear sticky material that, at close range, can immobilize ants within seconds.

Tube-forming termites are easily recognized by their careful construction work: they build mud tunnels and plasterwork around food sources such as dead sticks, stalks of grass, or the decaying trunks of desert trees. Inside the adobe walls, constructed of soil grains and fecal material cemented by saliva, the pale, defenseless workers feed on dead plant cells, protected from the harsh climate and from predators, including birds, insects, and lizards.

Unlike carpenter ants, termites don't just chew through wood. With the aid of microorganisms that live in their guts, they actually eat the wood, turning the cellulose—the part most animals simply can't digest—into edible sugars. Termites are far more efficient at eating cellulose than mammalian ungulates, such as cows; in fact, they thrive on the uneaten cellulose in cowpies.

Termites' eating habits are crucial to the continuation of life in arid climates. With little moisture, few of the recyclers familiar from wetter climates—such as molds, mosses, or earthworms—can survive in the deserts; rot is thus slow or nonexistent. (In the desert, cars don't rust, corpses dry out instead of decaying, and wood just dries out and bleaches.) Without termites' fertile excretions, the nutrients necessary for plant growth—and thus animal life—would remain locked up in dead plant tissues.

Hence the importance of termites and their symbiotic stomach fauna. Chewing their way through dead plants, these tiny creatures are responsible for most of the recycling of carbon and other nutrients in deserts and desert grasslands, says ecologist Walter G. Whitford. In fact, says Whitford, without termite's voracious appetites, the desert would drown in undecayed woody material. Cowpies alone would cover one-fifth of the desert surface in just fifty years.

Once I carefully lifted up a piece of a tube-forming termite tunnel, curious to see its inhabitants. The soft, pigmentless bodies of the exposed termites looked pale and vulnerable, like cave-dwelling creatures. I quickly replaced the protective covering. As I did, I was struck by how amazing it is that these tiny creatures, working in concert, can have such an enormous impact on the desert.

FAIRY SHRIMP

Camaronito
Streptocephalus texanus

With about two inches of precipitation, the playa comes to life. For in the mud lie seeds, spores, eggs, and estivating adult invertebrates, waiting for water and rehydration to swirl into activity. A flooded playa has a wealth of living crustaceans, insects, phytoplankton, and algae—all furiously reproducing as quickly as they can. As the temporary lake dries, ... the playa community retreats into the mud to wait once more.
—Stephen Trimble, THE SAGEBRUSH OCEAN

NAME: Fairy shrimp get their name from their appearance—miniature, transparent shrimp. *Camaronito*, in Spanish, means "tiny shrimp." *Streptocephalus*, "twisted head" in Greek, describes the queerly crumpled antennae which characterize males of this genus; *texanus* commemorates where they were first described.

SIZE: Adults range from one-eighth to three-eighths of an inch long

COLOR: Transparent to slightly greenish or pinkish, depending on the color of their food

RANGE: From the Colorado Plateau and the western Great Plains south into México

HABITAT: Ephemeral pools, potholes, and ponds in deserts and grasslands, from sand dunes to suburban lots.

One May, writes Uwe George in his book *In the Deserts of This Earth*, a park ranger driving his regular tour through the Mojave Desert in Southern California discovered a lake flooding a basin where, until a rainstorm a few days before, no water had been recorded for 26 years. He was astonished to find that the warm, shallow waters of this instant lake contained millions of tiny shrimplike creatures. The ranger emptied his canteen and collected a sample of the water with its mystery animals. When he returned less than a month later, the basin was bone dry; the lake and all signs of its inhabitants had vanished as completely as a mirage.

The enigmatical creatures were branchiopods—fairy shrimp and their cousins, tadpole and clam shrimp—miniature crustaceans called "foot-breathers" for the gills on their legs. These improbable beings materialize as soon as water floods a dry playa or fills a *tanque*—a bowl in the rock, and then disappear without a trace when their watery world dries up.

Although other creatures have adapted to the difficult conditions of ephemeral puddles and pools, fairy shrimp are found *only* in such inconstant—and thus inhospitable—waters. (Except for one *camaronito* that lives in the equally difficult and highly saline environment of the Great Salt Lake.) These habitats are born in abundance, flush with oxygen and nutrients washed in with the influx of water. But with the water comes a population explosion of other aquatic colonizers—from microscopic algae to spadefoot toad tadpoles. These instant inhabitants quickly deplete the life-giving resources and eat each other. As the water evaporates, concentrations of salts and other compounds rise. From hot midday to chilly night, water temperatures rise and fall as much as 30 degrees. If water from new rain or snowmelt floods in, it may replenish the supply of oxygen and nutrients, but it also causes wild fluctuations in temperature, water chemistry, and other crucial parameters of aquatic life. In the ever-changing world of ephemeral pools, there is only one constant: the aquatic habitat will eventually vanish.

The temporary nature of this habitat is not unusual for the desert. The unpredictable, sparse nature of precipitation in the desert means brief periods of staggering abundance, followed by much longer periods of absolute want. Many desert lives have evolved to take advantage of the fleeting plenty. Annual plants gamble that they can sprout, bloom, and set seed in the space of several weeks before the soil dries out. Amphibians such as spadefoot toads emerge, reproduce, and bet that their young can mature before the puddles vanish. The rains call forth insects by the score, from mosquitoes to termites, to begin new generations which may or may not survive until the next rain. And grazers and predators of all kinds, from pronghorn antelope to giant desert centipedes, schedule their reproduction to capitalize on the copious—but evanescent—quantities of food.

Fairy shrimp, however, take the strategy of exploiting ephemeral abundance to extraordinary lengths, materializing instantly with the sudden appearance of desert pools and vanishing as completely as the water does. Further, *camaronitos* exploit extreme environments that less-flexible opportunists such as spadefoot toads shun, from water-filled potholes in solid rock to shallow, slightly saline playa lakes in desert basins. Where do these curious crustaceans come from, and where do they go?

Fairy shrimp hatch within hours of puddle formation from long-lived eggs that persist in cracks in the soil. *Camaronitos* reproduce both asexually and sexually, bearing two entirely different kinds of eggs depending on the environmental conditions. When water and food are plentiful, these tiny creatures go for speed and numbers: they simply clone themselves, bringing forth thin-shelled, quickly developing "summer" eggs. These hatch within several days, mature in about two weeks, and are exact replicas of their mothers. Since each female fairy shrimp can bear tens or hundreds of eggs within her few-week life, the result is a veritable population explosion.

However, as the pond or puddle becomes more crowded, polluted by fecal matter and increasing concentrations of dissolved salts and other minerals, and as its temperature rises—all indications that their once-fecund watery world is disappearing—the tiny female crustaceans undergo hormonal changes. Their reproductive efforts shift from simple productivity to long-term survival of the species: now they lay eggs that hatch both females *and* males. The catastrophic environmental signals have an aphrodisiac effect on the new generation: mating fervor dominates. Males pursue females with a frenzy. Once they mate, the two *camaronitos* may remain attached for hours, dipping and swirling in a graceful aquatic ballet. The result is a second kind of egg, designed for persistence. These thick-walled "winter" or "resting" eggs, each the size and color of a grain of sand, can survive temperatures far below freezing, as well as broiling heat and complete desiccation. Although the fairy shrimp die and vanish, their dried out shells blown away on the next wind, the resting eggs live on in the dry puddle bottom, waiting for the moisture that will bring them to life.

Camaronitos hatch and mature in about fifteen days, progressing through a series of molts. A full-grown fairy shrimp is sheathed in a suit of transparent armor—its hard, outer skeleton—and swims on eleven pairs of flattened legs, using its long, slender, forked abdomen as a rudder. Female fairy shrimp possess a pair of long antennae; males, two short, kinked antennae for grasping their intended during mating. These miniature crustaceans scull through puddles and ponds on their backs, breathing through gills on their fluttering legs. The synchronous, wavelike motion of their legs pushes food — microscopic algae, protozoans, and detritus — in a continuous stream to the fairy shrimps' mouths.

Fairy shrimp seem to vanish with the last of the water when their ephemeral homes dry up. But their sand-grain-sized resting eggs live on, season after season, ready to burst into instant life with the next desert rain or snowmelt. Eggs collected at that playa lake in the Mojave Desert are now stored in a laboratory. One hundred years from the month the lake filled, scientists will add water and wait, hoping to witness the miracle of fairy shrimp.

AUTUMN

Autumn is a dry season in all four deserts. Drought—not freezing temperatures—draws the line between summer and winter, ending the growing season. The summer monsoon rains quit, and winter storms haven't yet begun to bless the deserts with their Pacific Ocean moisture. High pressure areas typically linger over the region, keeping skies clear and dry, and temperatures relatively warm. In fact, daytime temperatures in the lower elevations of the Mojave and Sonoran Deserts often climb into the eighties and sometimes the nineties through November. Only in the Great Basin Desert and at higher elevations does autumn bring cold temperatures—and snow.

As soils dry out, annual plants die and perennial plants shut down for the winter. Desert animals, as well, prepare for lean times—some, like harvester ants and kangaroo rats, stash stores of seeds; others, like desert tortoises and western diamondback rattlesnakes, reduce their activity or hibernate. Many, like Costa's hummingbirds and Scott's orioles, move away altogether until water returns to revive the deserts. Some simply move from cold northerly deserts to warm southerly ones: sage thrashers, for instance, forsake the Great Basin Desert in winter for the warmer Mojave, Sonoran, and Chihuahuan Deserts. While summer residents are preparing for drier, colder times ahead, other animals are migrating through or into the deserts to take advantage of their relatively mild winters. Winter residents sometimes move into niches vacated by summer residents: after Swainson's hawks head south to winter on the South American pampas, for instance, rough-legged hawks migrate in to take their places for the winter.

Autumn is a restless time in the desert, as each summer's crop of young ones roams in search of a home of its own. From coyotes and badgers to desert night lizards and digger bees, these newly grown-up animals must find their own niches—hunting, feeding, and breeding spaces in which to live out the days of their lives. Many don't survive the transition between cared-for youngster and self-supporting adult; instead, they become food for other desert residents.

Fall is a time of subtle changes for desert plants, a slow bleaching under the still-warm sun. But here and there, where permanent water sources or cooler climates nurture deciduous trees, autumn splashes the landscape with bright colors. Search out springs, streams, and rivers, or trek to mountain canyons and high plateaus. Look for brilliant gold colors where cottonwood forests still line desert rivers, including the Hassayampa in central Arizona and the Gila River in western New Mexico. Visit the canyons of the Guadalupe and Chisos Mountains of West Texas, where bigtooth maples turn intense scarlet, like exploding fireworks. Vivid yellow aspens and rusty orange Gambel's oaks splotch whole mountainsides in the Great Basin and the plateaus of southwestern Utah. It takes persistence to find brilliant autumn colors in the deserts, but the results are all the more rewarding for their rarity.

SACRED DATURA

Toloache
Datura wrightii

> The Jimsonweed blooms in the cool of the evening —one moonlit night at the Ranch I counted one hundred and twenty-five flowers.... When I found that they are poisonous, I dug them up but in Abiquiu a few keep growing persistently. Now when I think of the delicate fragrance of the flowers, I almost feel the coolness and sweetness of the evening.
> —Georgia O'Keeffe, GEORGIA O'KEEFFE

NAME: Sacred datura refers to the religious uses of this plant. *Toloache,* the plant's Spanish name, comes from an Aztec phrase translated as "I bow my head to you." *Datura* may come from an East Indian name for the plant; *wrightii* commemorates Charles Wright, who preserved the first specimen in the 1840s while walking 700 miles across west Texas, collecting plants.

SIZE: The mound of leaves grows up to five feet tall and equally wide; the trumpet-shaped blossoms are six inches long; the prickly fruits are two inches in diameter

COLOR: Flowers white with a lavender tinge

RANGE: From Texas across the Southwest to central California, north to Utah and Nevada, and south into México

HABITAT: Throughout the deserts from 1,000 feet to 6,500 feet elevation; especially noticeable along roadsides

NOTES: Although the flowers exude a delicious lemony fragrance, the whole plant is *very* poisonous. Another name, jimsonweed, a contraction of "Jamestown weed," commemorates an incident in 1676 at Jamestown, Virginia, were soldiers ate a related datura and nearly died.

When the earth was still soft, say the Zuñi of northwestern New Mexico, and things now impossible could happen, two curious children, brother and sister, found their way into the home of the gods. When the two returned to their own world, according to the story recorded in 1915 by anthropologist Matilda Coxe Stevenson in "Ethnobotany of the Zuñi Indians," they chattered indiscreetly about the secrets they had learned: how they "could make one sleep and see ghosts, and how they could make one walk about a little and see one who had committed theft." The Twin War Gods were deeply disturbed when they learned that the children were incautiously revealing sacred knowledge, and promptly caused the two to be swallowed up by the earth. At the spot where the children disappeared, the Zuñi say, plants sprouted, bearing beautiful, fragrant flowers just like the ones the brother and sister had worn in their hair.

Sacred datura, the plant that sprung from the spot where the children were swallowed up by the earth, can indeed make one sleep and see ghosts, to say nothing of walking about and having any number of visions. This common member of the Solanaceae, or potato family, contains powerful alkaloids in high concentrations, including atropine, the major component of belladonna. Eating even small amounts of any part of the plant can cause dizziness, dimmed sight, hallucinations, delirium, convulsions, and death.

This powerfully poisonous plant is one of the main drug plants used by the indigenous inhabitants of North and Central America. Pastes and teas made by soaking or steeping the leaves and seeds were used to induce visions and for divination, as an anesthetic for setting bones and to dull pain of all kinds, and to prevent miscarriage. But it was sacred datura's hallucinogenic properties that gave the plant its spiritual value—and that got the children in trouble back when the world was still soft. So great was their respect for the power of this plant, says Charles Francis Saunders in *Western Wildflowers and Their Stories*, that Aztec priests kept the seeds (which have the highest concentrations of alkaloids) in special containers and burned candles in front of them, consulting the seeds like oracles.

Curanderas, traditional *mejicano* herbal healers, still use sacred datura or *toloache* in external treatments. When added to bathwater, the leaves and flowers are said to relieve arthritis pain and muscle strains of all kinds. *Toloache* leaves are also mixed with lard for a salve to treat painful skin swellings. Note, however, that sacred datura is used very cautiously and only externally, where its alkaloids cannot enter the body in any way.

Sacred datura is not unique in the potato family in possessing narcotic properties: the family also includes belladonna, tobacco, henbane, and nightshade. Ironically, the same plant family includes some of our most important food plants, including eggplants, potatoes, and tomatoes. Both of the latter, like sacred datura, are indigenous to the New World. When Spanish explorers brought tomatoes back home, Europeans were initially reluctant to eat the exotic fruits, which resemble the berries of their deadly relative, nightshade.

Sacred datura is easy to spot, especially along roadsides and dry washes in the deserts. It is a perennial plant which sprouts each spring from a thickened taproot, growing a mound of stems covered with grayish or bluish green leaves, and dies back to the ground in winter. Large datura plants can reach five feet tall and at least that much across.

On summer and fall evenings, datura reveals its ethereal beauty when its huge, trumpet-shaped flowers, white tinged with lavender, open atop the plant. The silky texture of the corolla seems to glow in the dark, hence another common name, moonflower. The flowers broadcast a delicate lemon fragrance on the night air, attracting sphinx moths and other pollinators to sip the sweet nectar hidden at the base of the long floral tube. Each blossom lasts but one night; by the time the sun is hot the next morning, sacred datura's beautiful trumpets have crumpled into sodden wads of lavender tissue. Fertilized ovaries grow into green fruit covered with hooked spines and bearing the deadly seeds. The fruit, about the size and shape of a crabapple, gives rise to another common name, thorn-apple.

Desert plants go to great lengths to keep from being consumed by the hordes of hungry grazers, from ants to mule deer. Plants cover themselves with bad-tasting waxes or stinging hairs, sprout formidable spines, or, as in the case of sacred datura, accumulate poisons in their tissues. Sacred datura's deadly alkaloids repel most grazers, except for the larvae of the aptly named striped datura beetle, a close relative of the potato beetle. Ann Zwinger in *Wind in the Rock* reports that the larva of this beetle "chews avidly" on the stems and leaves of datura. But, says Zwinger, the little insect is apparently not immune to the alkaloids; the larvae are sometimes poisoned by their chosen food.

Sacred datura's ability to accumulate alkaloids for its own protection may make it useful in protecting the environment. Researchers at Los Alamos National Laboratory and New Mexico State University noticed that sacred datura and one of its relatives, ground cherry, flourished on contaminated blast sites at the laboratory. They are now studying whether the plants may be able to cleanse soils poisoned by nitro-based toxins, thus preventing the toxins from polluting the groundwater.

One morning in autumn, my newspaper carried a story about three teenagers who had brewed a tea of sacred datura during a party in the desert, hoping to take a hallucinogenic trip. Tragically, the three teens did "take a trip." Two died that night. The third staggered home hours later, delirious, his tongue stuck to the roof of his mouth. As the teenagers learned, and as the Zuñi say in the story from back when the world was still soft, sacred datura is a powerful plant. Like the desert itself, it demands respect for its deadly potential *and* its ethereal beauty.

DESERT TARANTULA

Tarántula
Aphonopelma chalcodes

Tarantulas, despite their fierce appearance, are not dangerous. Their venom produces less pain than a bee sting, and it takes some doing to get bitten by one.

—Jeremy Schmidt, A NATURAL HISTORY GUIDE: GRAND CANYON

NAME: *Tarantula* in English and *tarántula* in Spanish both commemorate the town of Taranto, in southern Italy, where a species of this big spider was first described. *Aphonopelma* means "pad-foot" in Greek, *chalcodes* is "copperlike," for the copper-colored, iridescent pads at the end of their legs.

SIZE: Body up to three inches across and legspan up to five inches in females; slightly smaller in males, body up to two inches and legspan of four inches

COLOR: Females brown with blond hair, males brownish black with reddish hair

RANGE: Mojave, Sonoran, and Chihuahuan Deserts, from Southern California to southern New Mexico, and south into México

HABITAT: Desert basins and foothills, wherever the ground is suitable for digging burrows

NOTES: Tarantulas are the largest spiders in North America. Females can live twenty-five years.

A tarantula looks like an arachnophobe's nightmare: an enormous spider with a stout, hairy body and eight furry legs that span the width of an adult human's hand—not to mention the fierce fangs, venom, and the four pairs of tiny eyes. In reality, however, these big spiders are mild-mannered creatures. They only bite if seriously provoked and their venom, designed for digesting prey, not hurting humans, is quite mild. Tarantulas are such harmless spiders, in fact, that they are often displayed in petting zoos and in educational demonstrations.

Although North American tarantula species are not confined to the deserts, these big spiders are well adapted to life in arid country. Desert tarantulas spend their days—and most of their nights, as well—in a burrow that they have carefully excavated in the soil. Lined with strands of spider silk, the burrow begins as a vertical shaft and then angles sideways, ending in a chamber about a foot below the soil surface. Insulated by the soil, a tarantula's home remains cool even on the hottest days, and, capped by a lid of spider silk, relatively humid as well. Tarantulas can survive in their tightly capped burrow for up to two years without food.

On summer and fall nights, tarantulas remove the silken lid and open their climate-controlled home for business: obtaining food. A tarantula hunts from inside its burrow. Unobtrusive lines of web silk run from the burrow to the ground outside, functioning like trip lines. When a passing creature hits the lines of silk, the vibrations alert the big spider and it rushes out to catch its meal, usually an insect or other arthropod, and sometimes another tarantula, a lizard, or a small rodent. A tarantula pounces on its prey, administering the coup de grace with its fangs. Then the spider regurgitates digestive fluid into the wound and waits until the soft parts of its prey have liquefied. The tarantula—unable to chew—sucks up its meal like a milkshake. When the big spider is finished, it returns to its underground den, leaving behind the empty shell.

Tarantulas spend so much of their lives in their burrows that they are not often seen. But from summer through fall, male tarantulas cruise the desert on all eight legs, looking for love. Their quest is a dangerous one: the larger females are as likely to eat, as to mate with, prowling males. When a male tarantula finds a female's burrow, he plucks the silken trip lines. She rushes out and rears, ready to pounce on a meal. He must quickly run under her, dodging her long, powerful legs, and grab her fangs with special hooks on the ends of his front legs. If he can thus immobilize her for long enough to insert one of his pedipalps, a pair of specially modified leglike front limbs, into her genital opening, he deposits his seminal fluid and mating is complete. But the male's life is by no means safe yet. He must withdraw his pedipalp, let go of her fangs, and run away before she can strike and kill him. Often the tip of his pedipalp breaks off and sticks in her genital opening. If so, he trades an appendage for mating success, because the broken-off limb blocks other males from mating with her. Tarantula mating is clearly not an enterprise for the faint-hearted, or the slow!

If the male desert tarantula successfully retreats without becoming his mate's meal, he skitters off in search of another mate. The female returns to her burrow and, the following spring, lays hundreds of eggs in a silken bag. She hangs the bag in her burrow and watches over it for seven weeks, until the spiderlings hatch. After hatching, the tiny tarantulas, looking just like miniatures of their mother, head off on their own. Most don't survive their first year: the young spiders are consumed by predators from lizards to roadrunners, pallid bats to coatimundis.

Desert tarantulas molt as they grow, shedding their skin every year. Tarantulas grow slowly, taking seven to ten years to reach full size and sexual maturity. Females may live twenty-five years; males, exposed to predation while searching for mates (and also often eaten by their intendeds), rarely live past their first mating season.

Besides their formidable fangs, desert tarantulas possess a unique defense: a patch of brittle, irritating hair on their abdomen. When threatened, a desert tarantula rapidly rubs its hind legs against its abdomen, working loose a cloud of hair which it kicks towards its assailant. The fine hairs sting the assailant's eyes and mucous membranes, distracting the predator until the tarantula can escape.

The largest wasps in the desert have evolved a tight predator-prey bond with these big spiders. Tarantula hawks, two-to-three-inch-long wasps with metallic blue black bodies and striking, bright orange wings, kill tarantulas to feed their young. The fight between the wasps and the much-larger and heavier spiders is a dramatic one. A female tarantula hawk lures a tarantula out of its burrow, probably by plucking the silken web lines. When the spider rushes out, the wasp hops on its abdomen and paralyzes the tarantula with one or more jabs of its half-inch-long stinger. The wasp then drags the comatose—but not dead—spider back into the burrow, crawls out from underneath it, lays an egg atop the tarantula's limp body, and seals the burrow. When the wasp larva hatches, it is provisioned with a cache of fresh meat—the comatose spider—to consume as it grows. After spending the winter in a pupa, it digs its way to the surface as a winged wasp the following spring.

A less well-known part of the tarantula hawk story is their mating game. Male tarantula hawks, similar to but smaller than females, cruise for mates by "hilltopping." They position themselves in a tree or shrub atop a hill or other vantage point, and scan the desert airspace, watching for passing females. (This behavior is comparable to a human male picking a barstool with a good view of the dance floor.) When a female tarantula hawk flies by, the first male to spot her gives chase, and, if she is willing, the two copulate briefly on the ground. Afterwards, they go about their separate business: he flies back to his post to scan the air for another potential mate; she heads off to feed on flower nectar and build up her strength for the perilous job of hunting tarantulas.

One afternoon not long after we moved to the desert, the biggest wasp I'd ever seen banged against my office window. She was as long as my thumb, with a shiny, blue black body and beautiful amber wings—a female tarantula hawk. In looking up her identity, I discovered her relationship with tarantulas and saw another piece of the intricate tapestry of relationships that make up desert life.

CALIFORNIA CONDOR

Cóndor
Gymnogyps californianus

I pray to the birds because I believe they will carry the messages of my heart upward. I pray to them because I believe in their existence, the way their songs begin and end each day—the invocations and benedictions of the Earth.

—Terry Tempest Williams, REFUGE

NAME: Condor comes from *cóndor*, the Spanish version of the Que-chan Indian name. *Gymnogyps* means "naked vulture" in Greek, a ref-erence to this bird's bare head and throat, *californianus*, "of California," is for their current range.

SIZE: Body is up to forty-five inches long, wings to 9½ feet from wingtip to wingtip, the largest wingspread of any North American land bird; weight, to twenty-five pounds

COLOR: Adults blue black with large white underwing patches, ju-veniles' plumage dark all over; adults' bare head is yellow or orange, juveniles', dark gray

VOICE: Hisses, grunts, coughs, and groans

RANGE: Until the late 1800s, from British Colombia south to Baja California, México; now confined to the San Gabriel Mountains north of Los Angeles and the Vermilion Cliffs of northern Arizona and southern Utah

HABITAT: Open country, from high mountains to desert

NOTES: The whooshing noise of a condor's wings can be heard up to half a mile away.

I t is a hot afternoon at the base of the thousand-foot-high wall of northern Arizona's Vermilion Cliffs. An enormous shape passes between you and the sun; its shadow slides away across the sandy ground. Another glides past. You look up and stand stock still. Two of the largest birds you have ever seen soar overhead, their black and white wings nearly twice as long as an adult human is tall.

These are California condors, the largest soaring birds in North America, and also the rarest. In 1996, the total population numbered just 121, most in captivity—only 17 lived free in the wild. California condors are vultures, members of the family Cathartidae, from the Greek word for "cleanser": they eat carrion—dead animals—thus disposing of potential sources of disease and controling parasite populations, as well as recycling the nutrients contained in the car-casses. Twice the size of the common turkey vulture or buzzard,

California condors are the undisputed giants of their kind in North America. In the scavenger pecking order, condors are near the top: when a condor arrives, turkey vultures, ravens, and other foragers wait their turn.

Condors spend their days soaring high in the air in search of food, flying a hundred miles or more in the doing. A fully grown California condor's immense wings and wide tail give it nearly thirteen square feet of loading surface, allowing it to soar at extremely slow speeds and thus stay aloft for hours without once beating its wings. By hitching a ride on a thermal—a rising column or bubble of warm air—or on the streams of wind, a soaring condor can rise as high as 15,000 feet in the air and glide as fast as sixty miles per hour. Like all soaring birds, condors float with their primaries—flight feathers—spread apart like the fingers on a hand. Adjusting the angle and tilt of each primary individually gives condors precise control of speed and flight direction, just like the flaps on an airplane wing. Airflow between the primaries counteracts the drag produced by their wide wings, reducing wingtip turbulence and lowering their stalling speed. The ability to ride the air to great heights and for great distances with little energy expenditure allows condors to survive on their randomly occurring and often widely dispersed food.

Once a condor spots a carcass in an open area of sufficient size for the huge bird to land and take off again—condors require about forty feet of runway space to lift their twenty-five-pound bodies into the air—it descends. On the ground, a condor is awkward, walking with a waddling gait, and looks positively repulsive as it rips into a dead animal, but these birds are elegantly adapted to their role as sanitarians. The bare skin of their heads and throats is easily cleaned after eating. Strong beaks and feet allow them to tear apart or move even the heaviest carcasses—four condors were once seen dragging off a hundred-pound dead grizzly bear. Sophisticated immune systems protect them from disease-causing organisms. Keen eyesight allows them to spot carcasses from great heights. After eating two to three pounds of meat, a condor is ready for bath time: the huge bird heads for a pond or stream, where it throws water over itself and carefully cleanses its skin and feathers of gore. Once clean and dry, a condor heads home to its roost high on an inaccessible canyon wall.

California condors are slow-growing, long-lived birds that don't reach sexual maturity until the winter of their seventh or eighth year, and may live three decades. Condor pairs court and mate in fall. After mating, they choose a nest site, a small cave or cleft high in a cliff face with a shelf that allows for easy takeoff and landing. In spring, the female lays a single, half-pound, five-inch-long egg on the floor of the cave. The parents brood the egg for about forty-two days before the baby condor, a hissing fluffball, hatches. For the next ten months, the parents bring home food for their growing child. Young condors stay with their parents until the summer of their second year, learning how to spot food and how to ride the streams of wind. Because of this lengthy adolescence, a condor pair breeds only every other year.

California condors are powerful, fearsome birds. In some American Indian cultures, they are revered as Thunderbird, a god whose mighty wings boom. Roger A. Caras tells one version of the story in *Source of the Thunder:* "The Tlingit people said the condor caused the thunder by flapping its wings.... The lightning, they claimed, came from the bird's red eyes. An angry condor, they were sure, was likely to create thunder and lightning until it was able at last to capture a whale to carry off to a mountaintop home."

When the Tlingits first told that story, California condors flourished across the western half of North America, and did, indeed, feed on whale carcasses. In 1602, Father Ascención, a Carmelite friar, described a flock feeding on a whale in Monterey Bay. At that time, condors dined on an abundant variety of carrion: bison, grizzly bears, whales, salmon, deer, and smaller creatures. In the past century or so, however, condors' food sources have been decimated, and condor populations have plummeted. The huge scavengers have been shot and their giant eggs "collected"; they have been poisoned by pesticides and predator control baits, and electrocuted on power lines. By 1982, only 21 California condors existed in the wild, all in a rugged canyon high above the Los Angeles basin.

To save these soaring giants, biologists launched a captive breeding program. Thirteen years later, with over 100 condors in zoos and nearly two dozen in the wild, they proposed starting a new population at the Vermilion Cliffs, a remote site near the Utah-Arizona border, north of the Grand Canyon. California condors soared over the area until the late 1800s. Nine young condors were ready, but local residents were not, fearing that the presence of an endangered species would hurt their region's economy. The project was postponed. Finally, on a December day in 1996, the doors of a pen holding six young condors were opened, releasing the giant birds to soar for their first time over the red wall of the Vermilion Cliffs. Whether these birds, raised in the Los Angeles Zoo, will survive in the lonely expanses of the Colorado Plateau has yet to be seen. But their release is a hopeful beginning.

Up a canyon in southern Arizona's Huachuca Mountains is a limestone cliff overhang chalked with pictographs. There, on the blackened rock ceiling, soar two birds with enormous wings outstretched: Thunderbirds, or California condors. I believe that California condors are necessary to the nourishment of the human spirit, like the sight of the Milky Way or the sound of saguaro needles singing in the wind. These things provoke awe—and perhaps fear. Awe and fear can be salutary emotions, reminding us that the universe is infinite and we, small. Crazy as it may seem, I pray to the condors, imploring them to return and grace the desert with their repulsive, awesome, necessary Thunderbird power.

FRÉMONT COTTONWOOD

Álamo
Populus fremontii

> *If there is magic on this planet, it is contained in water.*
> —Loren Eiseley, THE IMMENSE JOURNEY

NAME: *Cottonwood* is for the cottony fluff that surrounds the air-borne seeds. *Álamo* means "cottonwood" in Spanish and is a component of many southwestern place names. *Populus* may come from the Latin expression *arbor populi*, "the people's tree"; *fremontii* honors John C. Frémont, a lieutenant in the U.S. Army Topographical Corps who led five expeditions to the West.

SIZE: Up to eighty feet tall with a single trunk as large as twenty-five feet around and a crown spread that may stretch more than 100 feet

COLOR: Trunk of old trees gray and deeply furrowed; heart-shaped leaves shiny green when new, golden in autumn

RANGE: Below 7,000 feet elevation from extreme west Texas to Southern California, north to Nevada, Utah, and southern Colorado, south into México

HABITAT: Grows in the *bosques* along streams, rivers, and around *ciénagas* or springs. Also planted along irrigation ditches and in yards.

To understand why desert people venerate cottonwood trees, you may need to spend a summer day in the open desert, far from the sight or sound of running water. When the glaring light has numbed your brain and the heat has parched your body, search out the green canopy of a cottonwood tree. Sitting in its cool shade, your back braced against its furrowed trunk, listening to the raindroplike rustling of its leaves, you may begin to understand *álamo's* magic.

Although these big trees thrive throughout the deserts, cottonwoods cannot survive without water: they grow only where the soil retains moisture much of the year. Early desert travelers learned to search for cottonwoods; their leafy canopies signaled the presence of water like green beacons. Even a lone tree in a seemingly dry wash will suffice. Dig in the wash near the base of the tree until you reach damp sand, and water will eventually fill the hole. No wonder our affinity for a tree that proclaims the presence of water in these arid landscapes: we are 98 percent water, by weight, and we cannot survive without the liquid either.

There is more to desert-dwellers' love of cottonwood trees than the trees' association with water, however. Cottonwood trees' leafy canopy is the most dense of any desert tree and thus provides the deepest, coolest shade. Even the sound of a cottonwood is soothing, like the patter of raindrops on a roof. Cottonwood leaves rustle continually, because they are stiff and waxy, and attached to the leaf stem at an acute angle, causing the leaf to vibrate in the slightest breath of air. Although cottonwood wood is soft and punky, it is valued, partly because wood is scarce in the desert, partly because of the trees' association with water. Cottonwood roots are favored by the Hopi for carving their kachinas, sculptures of supernatural beings. Cottonwood trunks and large branches are hollowed out for two-headed ceremonial Pueblo drums. Navajos use cottonwood twigs for prayer sticks, and the branches and trunks for frames for rug looms, and hogan logs.

Frémont cottonwoods are broad-leafed cottonwoods, with nearly heart-shaped leaves, as wide as they are long. These fat-trunked trees begin as a tiny seed floating on a cloud of downy fluff as light as a snowflake. When cottonwood trees loose their thousands of seeds, drifts of white fluff fill the air in summertime blizzards. The seed must land on damp soil to sprout and only survives its first year if its fast-growing root can tap a source of perennial moisture. After studying cottonwood forests along desert rivers and streams, researchers think that the trees become established after floods. The seeds—which float equally well on water as on air—are carried out to the farthest margins of the floodwaters and left behind as the water recedes, along with a fertile wash of silt and nutrients.

Once its roots tap water, a cottonwood grows quickly, shooting up as much as fifteen feet a year. As the tree matures, its branches spread into a wide, rounded crown, its trunk thickens, and its bark splits into deep furrows, as if scratched by an angry bear. Frémont cottonwood grows as tall as ninety feet, with a truly awesome girth and crown spread. The largest known Frémont cottonwood, growing in western New Mexico, boasts a crown spread of 102 feet and an enormous trunk thirty-eight feet around—nearly twelve feet in diameter!

Cottonwoods are the most distinctive part of the unique *bosques* or riparian woodlands that line desert rivers and streams, and ring springs, and *ciénagas* (marshes, from "hundred waters" in Spanish). These riparian ecosystems are lush oases that, when compared to the surrounding desert, seem as dense and colorful as tropical jungles. Indeed, they support the most plants and animals per square foot of any desert habitat. Cottonwood trees alone furnish homes or food for hundreds of kinds of creatures. Their broad branches support the nesting platforms of colonies of great blue herons and egrets, and the solitary nests of ravens, vultures, and hawks. Holes formed in their soft wood when branches fall shelter owls, raccoons, ringtails, feral honeybee hives, and other cavity-nesters. Orioles hang their pendulous nests from the upper branches where yellow-billed cuckoos gorge on tent caterpillars. When their massive trunks fall, cottonwoods feed and shelter a whole new set of lives.

Cottonwood trees, like the water that sustains them, are scarcer in the desert today than a century ago. Maps of the Southwest are speckled with an even rain of water names: Stovepipe Wells, Hueco Tanks, San Simon Ciénaga, Alamogordo ("fat cottonwood"), Tularosa and Carrizozo (both meaning "place of the tules or reeds"), Ojo Caliente ("warm 'eye,'" or "waterhole"). Some of these still hold water; tragically, most don't. Over 90 percent of the desert's riparian communities, the water-loving plant and animal communities that once lined rivers and streams and ringed waterholes and marshes have disappeared, gone as the water dried up.

Where did the water go? A catastrophic combination of beaver elimination in the early 1800s, livestock overgrazing in the late 1800s, and fire suppression through the late 1900s drastically altered streamflow, causing once-permanent streams to dry up or to fluctuate widely between flood and trickle. Dams built to control river flooding and supply a steady source of water for agricultural irrigation further tinkered with stream and river flows. After World War II, cheap electricity and improved pumping technology allowed irrigators to tap groundwater, drying up *ciénagas* and *ojos* as water tables dropped precipitously.

Salt cedar, or tamarisk, a small tree introduced for erosion control and windbreaks by the U.S. Department of Agriculture beginning in 1899, wreaked further havoc on desert riparian communities, crowding out native plants, adding salt to desert soils, and sucking up scarce water. Salt cedar now dominates a million acres of riparian areas in the West and guzzles an estimated 5 million acre-feet of water each year. Its effect on stream and groundwater flows is dramatic. After a thicket of salt cedar grew up around a spring pond on the Pecos River of southeastern New Mexico, the pond, once a popular swimming hole, dried up completely. When the trees were killed, the pond—dry for nearly fifty years—filled again.

I love cottonwood trees best in autumn. Fall slips across the lower elevations of the desert country quietly, bringing a gradual diminution of summer's heat, but no colorful fireworks—except where *álamos* remain. The decreasing day length of autumn triggers cottonwoods to prepare for winter. They cease producing chlorophyll and its green pigments, and eventually drop their leaves. For me, the magic comes as the green pigments break down and the underlying pigments show through. Then, cottonwood's waxy leaves turn vibrant gold, flaming bright to signal another desert autumn.

RIVER OTTER

Nutria de la plata
Lutra canadensis

> *The otter is well-known as a good-natured clown, capable predator, fun-loving mammal that appears to be part fish. Everybody loves a river otter.*
>
> —Gary Turbak, SURVIVORS IN THE SHADOWS

NAME: *Otter* comes from the Greek *hydra,* or "water snake." *Nutria de la plata* means "otter of the river" in Spanish. *Lutra* is Latin for "otter"; *canadensis* means "of Canada," where these otters were first described.
SIZE: Adults three to four feet long, including over a foot of heavy tail; weight, ten to twenty-five pounds
COLOR: Rich chocolate above with a silvery sheen below
VOICE: Soft whistles and chirps
RANGE: Once found from the lower Colorado River north throughout North America; in the deserts now only known from a few streams in northern Nevada, Arizona, Utah, and western Colorado
HABITAT: Freshwater rivers, streams, marshes, and lakes
NOTES: River otters are aquatic members of the weasel family.

When I visit the Arizona-Sonora Desert Museum west of Tucson, Arizona, I always stop by the outdoor river exhibit, where a tall cottonwood with rustling leaves overhangs a stream of water dropping into a deep pool surrounded by rounded boulders. I hang over the railing of the bridge spanning the pool and search the clear water for otters. If I am lucky, a sinuous brown body cleaves the water below. This time I am, and I spot one, diving deep, its body undulating to propel itself, followed by a trail of silvery bubbles. The otter reaches the end of the pool and turns in a fluid somersault like a racing swimmer. It surfaces and pushes a cottonwood leaf across the pool like a tiny boat with its black nose, only its sleek head protruding from the water.

River otters play. A single otter, like the one I watched, may entertain itself by pushing a stick or leaf across the water's surface, or by dropping pebbles and diving to retrieve them. A group of otters, whistling and chirping, may chase one another through the water, dunk each other, and wrestle. *Nutrias* are known for their slides: a group gathers atop a mud- or snowbank, and one by one the otters hurtle down on their bellies like body surfers, sliding into the water.

Even the most cautious of biologists acknowledges these behaviors as play. River otters seem to simply enjoy having fun.

These mammals are at home in the water. *Nutrias* can swim right side up, upside down, on their side, or any way. They propel themselves swiftly and gracefully through the water by undulating like fish, using their heavy tail as a rudder. They can execute sudden U-turns, dive as deep as forty feet, and spin in somersaults. River otters' legs are short but strong and their toes are webbed for better propulsion. Their streamlined bodies—up to four feet long, including as much as a foot-and-a-half of tail—are covered in thick, water-repellent fur. Dense, oily underfur traps air, keeping them warm even in near-freezing water. Their nostrils and ears close underwater, helping them remain submerged for several minutes.

On land, river otters lope along on short legs. On snow or ice, they speed along by sledding on their bellies: they run forward, then flop down and glide with an occasional push from their powerful hind legs.

Despite their clownlike antics, river otters are—like all members of the weasel family—accomplished predators. Their aquatic agility and speed allow them to compete with Colorado squawfish, northern pike, and other swift fish-eating fish, chasing and consuming swimmers from shiners to trout. River otters also dine on other aquatic life, including frogs, turtles, snakes, and crayfish.

Nutrias are gregarious animals, and are usually seen in pairs or family groups. Like their weasel relatives, they are territorial. A male's territory, marked with scent from his musk glands, may be as large as fifteen miles across; females' territories are smaller. (Males and females live apart.) River otters mate between March and May, just after the female has given birth to a litter of one to four babies conceived the previous spring. As with bears, implantation of the embryo is delayed until the following spring. Thus, otters mate when abundant food supplies ensure both parents are well-nourished, but delay pregnancy and its demands until after the female has reared the current batch of young and survived the winter. The babies are born helpless, toothless and with their eyes closed, and are raised by their mother until after weaning, at four months of age. They stay with their family group until winter, then head off to stake their own territories. River otters appropriate abandoned dens of bank beavers or other animals, and sometimes simply nest on the ground on hummocks in marshes.

River otters once swam in rivers, streams, and large marshes throughout the northern desert region, and in the Colorado River as far downstream as Yuma, Arizona. But by 1840, fur trappers had nearly exterminated beaver and river otters from the entire West. During a two-week trapping spree in 1825 on the San Francisco River in New Mexico, for instance, trapper James Ohio Pattie wrote that he and his six colleagues trapped *one thousand* beaver. Beaver removal tolled the death knell for any *nutria* that survived trapping. Beaver ponds and dams catch sediment, stabilize river flows, and create marshes, all crucial conditions for otter survival. Subsequent careless mining, logging, and livestock grazing exacerbated the damage. By the mid-1900s, river otters had nearly vanished from the Southwest. Although they have been reintroduced in some drainages, their progress is slow. Shoreline development, water pollution, and the continuing de-watering of desert rivers wreak havoc on potential *nutria* habitat.

When I stop to watch the river otters play at the Arizona-Sonora Desert Museum, I notice the responses of the other observers. Most peoples' bodies relax as they lean over the railing or peer through the underwater window, their faces breaking into smiles and grins. The joy in otter play seems contagious. As I walk the rivers and streams of the desert's mountains, I search for otters, hoping that we can re-create the conditions they need. In my vision of the future, river otters frolic, dive, and slide home to bless the desert's precious running waters.

PALLID BAT

Murciélago pálido
Antrozous pallidus

It beggars my imagination to think how something so small can be so complex. I think of all the things that it can do that I cannot, of what I know that it does not, and of what we share, a common chromosome perhaps, or a retinal cell.

—Ann Haymond Zwinger, THE MYSTERIOUS LANDS

N A M E : Pallid bats are named for their blond fur. *Murciélago* is "bat" in Spanish, *pálido* comes from the Latin *pallidus,* or "pale." *Antrozous* is Greek for "cave animal."

S I Z E : Adults' wingspan is fourteen to fifteen inches, their bodies are just 2½ to 3 inches long, and they weigh less than an ounce—about the same as a candy bar

C O L O R : Fur pale—blond above, whitish below; exposed skin of ears and nose pink, wing membranes pink with a blue black cast

V O I C E : High squeals and chirps at the margin of the range of human hearing

R A N G E : Below 6,000 feet elevation from México north through the arid West to British Columbia, isolated colonies on the western Great Plains in Kansas and Oklahoma

H A B I T A T : Open desert and grassland; roosts in rock crevices, caves, and under roofs of open buildings

N O T E S : Bats are the only flying mammals. (Flying squirrels glide through the air, but cannot actually fly under their own power.)

Have you ever held a bat in your hand? I did one evening, and I fell in love. She chattered in a high-pitched voice, then nestled her warm body comfortably in my closed hand. I was astounded by how small her body was—not much larger than an unshelled walnut. Her head barely protruded over my thumb. I stroked her soft fur with one fingertip as her large, dark eyes watched my face. I listened to her heartbeat through a stethoscope: at her resting rate of 600 beats per minute, her heart pulsed so fast that the individual beats overlapped like the drops of rain in a spring storm.

Pallid bats spend their days resting out of sight in a shallow cave or wedged in a crevice in rocks or a building. Resting, for a bat, means hanging upside down by the claws in their feet, lowering their heart rate, and snoozing. When it is completely dark, these *murciélagos* drop from their perches, and flutter off to hunt. They fly low across open country, listening for the low frequency sounds made by ground-dwelling insects. Most desert bats feed on the wing, either scooping insects out of the air or hovering to drink nectar from plants; pallid bats light on the ground or land on plants to capture their meals: insects, scorpions, centipedes, small lizards, and small rodents.

Pallid bats locate their prey by sight—contrary to popular understanding, bats are not blind—and by using their sophisticated echolocation systems. The squealing and chattering that I heard when I held the pallid bat was simply the low frequency end of its sound range. Pallid bats' big ears, with their tragus, an odd upright flap directly in front of each ear opening, serve as sensitive antennae, picking up sound waves that bounce off of surrounding objects. Echolocation allows a bat to "hear" in total darkness with such precision that it can perceive objects as fine as a single human hair.

Like many desert animals, pallid bats conserve water: they can survive without it for long stretches of time by metabolizing water from their food. Pallid bats have survived up to a month in captivity without drinking water.

Pallid bats are colonial, spending their days and their winters roosting with a dozen to a hundred other pallid bats. In winter, these *murciélagos* hibernate in groups in rock crevices or caves. During hibernation, they drop their heart rates to as low as one beat per *minute* and can survive incredibly low body temperatures—some species' internal temperatures can drop as low as 20 degrees! But pallid bats aren't out cold all the time: sometime between October and February, they mate. The female stores the male's sperm until April, when she emerges from hibernation.

Her one or two babies are born in June, and raised in a nursery roost with other mother pallid bats and their babies. (Bats, like primates, have only two nipples, and so cannot nurse more than two young at a time.) The female gives birth upside up—that is, hanging with her head up, not hanging head down, as usual—catching the babies in the "basket" formed by her upcurved tail membrane. The babies cling to their mother's fur with their thumblike claws except when she is out hunting. The little *murciélagos* are ready to fly when they are five or six weeks old.

Pallid bat nursery roosts of twenty to 100 bats are comparatively small for colonial bats—one Mexican free-tail bat nursery roost in Texas, for example, numbers up to 20 *million* baby bats. How do free-tail bat mothers, returning to the roost after a night's feeding, locate their own baby among the millions clustered together on a cave roof? Each mother, it seems, can pick out her own baby's voice in the din. Astoundingly, says bat biologist Donna Howell, the mothers rarely err. And if they do, she says, they invariably chose the baby of a close relative.

Roosting en masse may give bats thermal protection and protection from predators. But roosts are vulnerable to human disturbance. In Phoenix, Arizona, for instance, two men shot and killed more than 500 Mexican free-tail bats roosting under a bridge. Even benign sightseeing endangers roosting bats: disturbance may cause mother bats to abandon nursery roosts—leaving their babies to starve. Bats roused from hibernation in winter consume from ten to thirty days of fat reserves by "waking up" and thus may exhaust their reserves and die before food is available in spring.

Bat populations are declining throughout North America, partly due to disturbance and partly due to pesticides. Insect-eating bats consume prodigious quantities of night-flying "pests" like mosquitoes and insects that eat crops. Biologists calculated that one bat colony near San Antonio, Texas saved area farmers several million dollars each year in pesticide costs by devouring insects that would otherwise consume their crops. Ironically, as bats efficiently eat insects, they also consume pesticides. The poisons accumulate in their body fat and then are metabolized, killing the bats as they draw on their fat stores in hibernation.

Bats deserve better. These tiny flying mammals not only consume literally tons of pest insects, they are also key pollinators of many desert plants, including agaves and saguaro cactus. Moreover, bats are simply extraordinary creatures. If you ever have a chance to hold a bat—as I did—take it. (Don't, of course, catch a wild bat. The *murciélago* I held, once badly injured, had been trained for human contact.) Stroke the bat's soft fur and listen to the storm of its heartbeats. Examine its beautifully engineered wings. And don't be surprised when you lose your heart.

CENTURY PLANT

Agave
Agave parryi

It has been said that century plants kill themselves reproducing—not a bad way to go, when you think about it. The obvious drawback is that after a rather dull, prolonged adolescence, they have only the energy to do it once.

—Gary Paul Nabhan, GATHERING THE DESERT

NAME: Century plant, the name given to large agaves because they were thought to bloom but once a century, is a misnomer, but these plants do bloom just once in their five- to fifty-year lives. *Agave* is from the Greek word for "noble"; *parryi* honors Charles Christopher Parry, a nineteenth-century botanist who traveled throughout the West.

SIZE: Leaf rosette up to two feet across and equally high, individual leaves up to eighteen inches long, thick and broad, and tipped with a stout spine; flower stalk to fourteen feet high

COLOR: Leaves blue green; flowers bright yellow, tubular, and pointing upward in dense clusters

RANGE: Below 7,000 feet elevation from central Arizona east to west Texas and south into central México

HABITAT: Well-drained soils of *bajadas* and mountainsides

NOTES: The flowers smell cloyingly sweet, like rotting meat.

Century plants, or *agaves*, live surprising lives. These large relatives of lilies spend their first several decades quietly growing a succulent rosette of stiff and leathery leaves in which they store food and water. But once mature—in as few as five years or as many as fifty, depending on the species and the growing conditions—they squander all their stores on one glorious burst of reproduction, then die. When they are ready to bloom, a flower stalk that looks just like an enormous asparagus sprouts from the center of the leaf rosette, growing as fast as a foot a day and eventually towering over the parent plant. (The flower stalks of some century plants grow thirty feet tall!) To fuel this extraordinary growth spurt, the plant literally uses itself up, sucking out all of the provisions stored in its leaves. A century plant with a leaf rosette two feet across loses about fifty-five pounds of water weight to grow a flower stalk twelve feet high. As the leaves begin to wither, horizontal branches sprout from the flower stalk and clusters of buds swell at the end of each branch. The buds open at night, revealing yellow, tubular flowers that point upwards and emit strong, musky fragrances, attracting night-flying pollinators. By the time its seeds have matured, the parent plant is gray, shriveled, dead.

Why would a plant risk its reproductive chances—and its life— on one big bang? As bat biologist Donna Howell discovered, century plants have evolved a special relationship with nectar-feeding bats. Two species of long-nosed bats migrate north just as the agaves bloom. The bats depend on the abundant nectar and pollen in the agave flowers; the big plants depend on the bats for cross-pollination. Century plants and other bat-pollinated plants, says Howell, have evolved floral characteristics that make it easy for bats to feed and, at the same time, service the plant's reproductive needs. First, the flowers themselves are large and open, enabling a bat to thrust its whole face into the flower to slurp nectar. Second, the flowers are located on tall pedestals that are easily detected at great distance on moonlit nights. Century plant flowers go even further: they smell like rotten meat, a scent attractive to bats; their nectar secretions peak between eight and ten o'clock at night when the bats are most active; and the nectar is high in the very nutrients that bats need. In effect, century plants risk it all on one throw of a die, betting all of their resources on one extravagant display in order to attract more bats and thus produce more seeds.

If staking all of their reproductive energy on one attempt is risky for the century plants, the relationship is equally hazardous for their partners in pollination, say Gary Paul Nabhan and Stephen L. Buchmann in *The Forgotten Pollinators*. The long-nosed bats travel a 3,200-mile-long, looping migration route from wintering caves deep in México to nursery roosts as far north as Tucson, Arizona, and Big Bend, Texas, and back again. This nectar corridor follows the sequential flowering of at least sixteen plant species, including tree morning glories, century plants, and columnar cacti like saguaros. Along the way, say Nabhan and Buchmann, the little bats must surmount great risks: pesticide poisoning, elimination of the nectar-producing plants that they depend on, and the dynamiting of their roosting sites.

Century plants and desert-dwelling humans also have a close relationship. The spiny-leafed plants once nourished desert-dwellers with *mescal*, roasted agave hearts, a seasonal food so important that it is still used ceremonially. (The name *mescal* is now used for an alcoholic beverage also produced from century plants.) *Mescal* pits—rock-lined pits built for roasting the young flower stalks and the succulent heart of the leaf rosette—are common desert archaeological sites, dating back as far as 8,000 years. The Hohokam of what is now central and southern Arizona cultivated century plants in specially designed fields as early as A.D. 1150. Today's Mescalero Apache of southern New Mexico are named for their historic trade in and diet of *mescal*. The big plants also supplied fiber for rope and cloth, and the makings for soap.

People in northern México still harvest and roast wild agaves— but not to eat. The sugary hearts are fermented to produce *pulque*, a bootleg liquor which can be distilled into tequila and mescal. Increasing populations in rural northern México plus increased demand for bootleg liquor equal a serious threat to wild century plant populations there and to nectar-feeding bats as well. Buchmann and Nabhan estimate that over one *million* wild century plants are harvested each year for bootleg liquor production in the Mexican state of Sonora alone. (Farm-grown century plants are the source of commercial tequila and mescal.) Not surprisingly, the elegantly evolved relationship between bat and century plant is fraying.

The first summer we lived in the desert, I noticed an enormous bud appearing from the leaf rosette of a century plant in a neighbor's yard. For several weeks, I watched with amazement as the giant stalk spurted upwards. Then came tragedy: just before it burst into bloom, someone felled the flower stalk with a chain saw. The plant that had produced it died soon after, having literally spent its energy fruitlessly. The fate of that agave, to me, symbolizes where humans err: we tinker with the desert without understanding the relationships that sustain that web of interlinked lives. To cut down an agave stalk before it can bloom; to sever the link between nectar-feeding bat and host plant—these actions betray our obtuseness, and may in the end, betray our future. In his essay "Round River," Aldo Leopold wrote: "If the land mechanism as a whole is good, then every part is good, whether we understand it or not.... To keep every cog and wheel is the first precaution of intelligent tinkering."

DESERT BIGHORN SHEEP

Borrego cimarrón
Ovis canadensis mexicana

> *Size DOES count.*
> —Bumper sticker on a monster truck, Silver City, New
> Mexico

NAME: Bighorn sheep are named for the males' massive curling horns. *Borrego cimarrón* in Spanish means "wild sheep." *Ovis* is Latin for "sheep"; *canadensis*, "of Canada," refers to where the species was first described; the subspecies name means "of México."

SIZE: Up to forty inches high at the shoulder; rams weigh up to 160 pounds, ewes to 110 pounds

COLOR: Pale brown to grayish brown above with white rump and muzzle

RANGE: West Texas north to southern Utah and Nevada, south to Baja California and mainland México

HABITAT: Rocky desert mesas and mountain ranges

For these tough *cimarrones*, size really does count. The bigger the male's headset, the higher his ranking in the old boys' club—the social order that determines a male bighorn's right to drink at waterholes, to feed at the choice spots, and to mate. Size also requires time: it takes seven or eight years to grow the full curl of a top-ranking ram, whose horns may measure thirty or more inches from base to tip.

Each fall, pairs of rams dispute the rankings in dramatic butting contests. First, two rams snort at each other and then back off until they are many yards apart. Then they rear up on their hind legs, drop down with heads lowered, and lunge at each other at high speed. Their foreheads collide with a loud *crack!* that can be heard for a mile. A double-layered skull enables these truly hard-headed sheep to withstand repeated collisions. The two back up and knock heads again and again, until one gives way. The victor moves up in the pecking order; the loser retires unharmed, except, perhaps, by the blow to his status!

The male's head-banging contests determine who gets to mate with the females in the herd. Adult bighorn sheep spend most of the year segregated by sex: males hang out together, females and young form separate nursery groups. The adults mix in fall, then split up again after mating. In spring, pregnant females go off alone to give birth to one or two lambs, then return within a few days to the protection of the nursery herd. The lambs are precocious, able to run and leap soon after birth. They begin grazing at about two weeks and are weaned by four to six months. Females begin mating in their third year; male *cimarrones* usually don't succeed in mating until they rise in the pecking order, which takes seven or eight years. But when they do, they make up for lost time by mating with as many females as they can.

Desert bighorn sheep inhabit some of the rockiest, sparest, most inaccessible habitats: from the sheer cliffs of the Colorado Plateau to the rocky slopes of the seemingly barren mountains of the lower deserts. Small, heavily muscled bodies and spongy, concave hooves allow *cimarrones* to negotiate rocky cliffs and precipitous slopes with agility, leaping as far as twenty feet from hoofhold to hoofhold. Bighorns can go for days without drinking water and can withstand severe dehydration, losing up to 20 percent of their body weight in water loss. (When humans lose over 10 percent of our weight in water, we drift into unconsciousness; we die after losing 12 percent.) They can rehydrate themselves quickly in a single visit to a waterhole: arriving emaciated, a bighorn may drink steadily for as long as ten minutes, then depart plump! If drinking-water sources dry up, *cimarrones* find water. In an essay in *Counting Sheep*, Doug Peacock reports seeing a dominant male carefully use his horns to break open the top of a fearsomely spined barrel cactus. He then ate the spongy innards, while his band stood around and waited their turn.

A complex digestive system also helps bighorn sheep survive in their harsh, arid habitats. *Cimarrones* are ruminants, grazing animals with multiple stomachlike fermentation vats that wring every last calorie and drop of water from their food. A trip through a bighorn's digestive system reduces the four pounds of grasses and shrub twigs that an adult eats each day to a handful of small, dry pellets. Chewed food goes first to the rumen, where bacteria help convert the cellulose to useable sugars, then to the reticulum for further digestion, then back to the mouth for rumination (more chewing). The food is then reswallowed and sent through four more fermentation chambers before passing through the large intestine, which removes the water. Bighorns' lengthy digestive process takes hours, hence our verb *ruminate*, "to meditate, think over slowly, to ponder."

Their rugged habitat protects bighorns from most predators—although mountain lions eat them occasionally—but not from human disturbance. When Francisco Vasquez de Coronado explored the desert Southwest from 1540 to 1542, he mentioned seeing "some sheep as big as a horse, with very large horns and little tails." At the time of Coronado's expedition, biologists estimate that 2 million *cimarrones* lived throughout western North America. By 1960, only 20,000—or about 1 percent of the original population—remained, including some 8,000 desert bighorns. (The eight subspecies of bighorn sheep are lumped into two types: mountain bighorns and desert bighorns. The former occupy high elevations in the Rocky Mountains; the latter, desert mountains and mesas.)

What happened to the native *cimarrones?* Ranchers introduced domestic livestock, pushing wild sheep from the best habitat and passing on diseases. Trophy hunters decimated whole herds. (Illegal hunting is still a problem. Not long ago, a headhunter shot the trophy-sized ram at a major zoo.) State game departments introduced exotic animals, displacing bighorns. The rest of us built houses and roads right up into desert mountain ranges, cutting off bighorns' migration routes and access to waterholes, and pushing these cautious animals into ever more remote territory. Despite captive breeding and aggressive re-introduction programs, populations of desert bighorns are still small, limited by the size and isolation of remaining "islands" of wild country.

When I feel despondent about the future of bighorn sheep—and humans—in the desert, I remember a ridge of dark volcanic rock that rises above a desert basin near my home. The rocks along the ridgeline are alive with thousands of images of fish, birds, insects, and mammals—including dozens of *cimarrones.* In some of these rock drawings the sheep are solitary, in others, in groups; some bighorns are studded with arrows, some leap freely from rock to rock. The pale images pecked into the dark desert varnish are carefully drawn; researchers say that many hours went into the creation of each image. That gives me courage. The creators of these petroglyphs seem to have revered the wild spirits of bighorns and other desert creatures. If we can learn to make space for bighorns in our desert lives, we too can leave a legacy that will show future generations — as the petroglyphs show us — that *cimarrones* are integral and necessary parts of our world.

GILA MONSTER

Monstruo de Gila
Heloderma suspectum

> *A typical day in the life of a Gila monster is not an exciting affair. It's basically 24 hours of sleep in a rocky crevice or burrow. The day spent resting might be punctuated with a few large breaths, a turn of the body here and there, and perhaps a tongue flick or two.... Gila monsters live life on the edge of slowness.*
>
> —Daniel D. Beck, "The Gila Monster in Southwestern New Mexico," SHARE WITH WILDLIFE

NAME: The English and Spanish names both mean the same thing: "Gila" for the Gila River, where they were first described; "monster" for these big lizards' fearsome appearance. *Heloderma*, "warty skin" in Greek, describes the texture of their skin; *suspectum* is from the Latin "to mistrust."

SIZE: Adults range from eighteen to twenty-four inches long, with heavy bodies and fat, sausagelike tails

COLOR: Black background crossed by mottled stripes in pink, orange, or yellow

VOICE: Hisses and grunts

RANGE: Near sea level to 4,100 feet elevation from extreme southwest Utah south to northern México, from the Colorado River east to western New Mexico

HABITAT: Canyon bottoms, arroyos, and near irrigated farms in grasslands or shrub deserts

NOTES: The Gila monster is our largest native lizard and one of only two venomous lizards in the world.

Walking down a desert wash, I rounded a corner and stopped abruptly. Atop a boulder directly in front of me was a truly enormous lizard. Its warty black and pink skin covered a body larger around than my forearm and nearly two feet long, with a fat, swollen tail and stumpy legs. The lizard opened its mouth, revealing a double row of sharp, pointed teeth, and hissed loudly. I involuntarily jumped backwards, startled by my first encounter with a Gila monster.

Gila monsters and their cousins, the Mexican beaded lizard, are the only two venomous lizards in the world. These two are the sole living species of a group of poisonous lizards that was once more widespread—but not recently. Their only relatives are, literally, fossils. Unlike the fancy hollow fangs of venomous snakes such as rattlesnakes, these *monstruos* rely on a very simple venom-dispensing method. They bite their victim with their sharp teeth and hold fast with a tenacious grip. As their teeth tear the victim's flesh, glands under the skin in their lower jaw secrete venom, which runs along grooves in the teeth and drips into the wound. Gila monster venom kills small animals by respiratory paralysis. In humans, the venom is severely painful, and causes swelling, nausea, and weakness—but is not fatal.

Gila monsters are deceptive. They look and sound horrific—but these *monstruos* are nine-tenths bluff and bluster. Their bright colors shout "Beware—I am venomous!" Their hissing stance and stout body say "Back off!" But a Gila monster's usual response to a threat is to lumber away. It bites only as a last resort. Says herpetologist Daniel Beck: "To get bitten, you practically have to stick your hand into the Gila monster's mouth."

It's not often one sees a Gila monster. These big lizards spend nearly all their lives—over 95 percent of their time, according to one study—snoozing in rock or earthen shelters. But Gila monsters move around through the year, picking their dens to suit the season: in winter, they select rocky crevices facing south or east to catch solar radiation. In spring, they opt for morning sun and afternoon shade. In summer's heat, the *monstruos*, like many other desert creatures, take to the earth in burrows that they dig themselves or in abandoned packrat mounds. Earthen burrows retain much higher humidity than rock crevices, helping the big lizards avoid dehydration during the desert's severest weather. *Monstruos* return to the same crevices and burrows year after year.

The fat stored in their sausagelike tails sustains Gila monsters as they snooze through the desert's extremes of climate. They bestir themselves in spring or after the summer rains, lumbering out to hunt only when food is likely to be easily obtained. Like chuckwallas and desert tortoises, Gila monsters take advantage of the relative abundance of food during the rainy season, then retreat to burrows and wait—sometimes for years—until food is plentiful again. *Monstruos* are picky eaters. Their taste runs to young and tender flesh: baby cottontails, ground squirrels, and baby birds; bird or tortoise eggs; and young lizards. When a *monstruo* finds suitable prey, it lunges forward and bites its victim, holds on until the victim stops struggling, then consumes its food. The big lizards stuff themselves—eating up to half their body weight in one meal—then waddle off to digest. Fat stored from one gluttonous binge can maintain a snoozing lizard for a year.

Female and male *monstruos* live separately for most of the year, but in spring, males search out females' dens. Unlike other lizards which use color and speed to prove their fitness as mates, these big, husky lizards wrestle. Pairs of Gila monsters square off and compete in grunting, ritualistic matches until one tires and wanders off. To the victor goes the opportunity to mate with nearby females.

In midsummer, a mated female Gila monster lays one to eight eggs in a hollow scooped out of moist sand in a wash bottom or near a stream or spring. The survival of the eggs depends not on her continuing attendance—she leaves after laying the eggs—but on her expertise in site selection. If she has picked a spot where the sun warms the soil but doesn't dry it out, the eggs develop. That fall or the next spring, three-inch-long baby *monstruos* dig upwards through the soil, and set off looking for food. Owls, coyotes, kit foxes, and rattlesnakes all eat baby Gila monsters. Those that survive can live long lives—up to twenty years in captivity.

When the Arizona state legislature passed a law in 1952 making it illegal to kill or collect Gila monsters, these fearsome lizards were the only venomous animals so protected. As with many desert lives, the greatest danger these days to Gila monsters' continuing survival is habitat destruction by humans. So far, though, these giants seem to be holding their own. I'm hoping that never changes. A desert without *monstruos* would be like a cactus without spines—no desert at all.

Mountain Lion

León
Felis concolor

Puma, cougar, catamount; Felis concolor, *the shy, secret, shadowy lion of the New World, four or five feet long plus a yard of black-tipped tail, weighs about what a woman weighs, lives where the deer live from Canada to Chile, but always shyer, always fewer, the color of dry leaves, dry grass.*

—Ursula K. Le Guin, "May's Lion," Buffalo Gals and Other Animal Presences

NAME: Mountain lions are also called cougar and puma; the former is an Andean name, the latter an Amazonian name. *León* in Spanish simply means "the lion." *Felis* is Latin for "cat"; *concolor* is Latin for one color, referring to the tawny coloring of these big cats.
SIZE: Up to seven feet from nose to tip of tail; males weigh up to 160 pounds, females to 130 pounds
COLOR: Tawny yellow above, belly whitish, tail black at tip; young spotted with black
VOICE: Purrs, hisses, meows, and screams like a mating tomcat
RANGE: Wild country throughout the Americas, from Patagonia to the Yukon
HABITAT: Variable over its wide range, includes desert mountains, mesas, swamps
NOTES: Mountain lions' eyes shine green in lights at night.

Early one August morning, a mountain lion was sighted in a suburb at the edge of my desert town. A homeowner called the police, who called the Game and Fish Department. By the time the officers arrived to search for it, all that remained were oversized cat tracks and scared dogs. The lion itself had vanished up an arroyo toward the nearby mountains.

Mountain lions are the soul of the Southwest's desert mountains and mesas. These big cats are secretive and rarely seen, but they make their presence known. The second largest cat in the Americas—only jaguars are larger—*leones* were once the most widespread wild cat in the Americas, ranging from the tip of South America to northwestern Canada, and from the Pacific Coast to the Atlantic. In North America, an all-out war on predators that began with European settlement has eliminated these graceful cats from much of the eastern part of their range. Only where large areas of rugged, relatively inaccessible country remain—including the desert regions—are mountain lions still plentiful.

American folklore is full of stories about *leones*: the blood-curdling screams that they supposedly utter just before they leap on their prey, their sensational ability to kill animals of any size, their penchant for tracking humans. In truth, these big cats are graceful and formidable hunters, but contrary to folklore, they hunt silently. Mountain lions prefer deer, but if deer are scarce, they will kill and eat any available live prey, from elk to calves to poodles to humans. *Leones* hunt like enormous house cats, stalking their prey with tails twitching. The resemblance fades, however, when the big cat puts on the power, rushing forward as fast as forty miles per hour and leaping onto the back of its victim. Once astride its prey, the mountain lion embeds its curving claws in the animal's flesh and bites the victim's neck with its oversized canine teeth, severing the victim's spinal cord with an audible *crack. Leones* also hunt by crouching motionless on a cliff ledge or tree branch above a deer trail. When dinner passes underneath, the big cat silently drops on its prey and kills it. Biologists estimate that an adult mountain lion needs to kill the equivalent of one deer a week to survive.

Leones do indeed sometimes stalk humans, and have been known to follow a person's tracks for many miles and never attack them. Recently, however, as people have moved in greater numbers up into the foothills and mesas that are prime *león* territory, human-lion encounters have become more common. In 1991, a mountain lion killed a teenaged jogger above Colorado Springs, Colorado. It was the first fatal encounter in many years. Since then, half a dozen other people have been killed by lions in California, Montana, Colorado, and British Columbia. To put those deaths in perspective, domestic dogs kill, on average, half a dozen people each year in the same region. The best way to avoid a lion attack is to not wander lion country alone. If you do encounter a *león,* say biologists, don't run. Stand your ground, look as big as possible, and make plenty of noise.

Adult *leones* are solitary animals except for the bond between a mother lion *and* her kittens, and brief mating liaisons. Males sleep around, staying with a given female only for the duration of her estrus. About three months after conception, female mountain lions give birth to two or three kittens in a sheltered place—for instance, an oak thicket, a brushy rockpile, or a shelter cave in a cliff.

Like all cats, young *leones* are born helpless, with their eyes shut tight. By the time they are two months old, however, they have begun to eat meat and to follow their mother to food. In fact, their mother may leave them at a fresh kill for several days while she hunts for their next meal. Mountain lions normally disguise their food by kicking dirt, leaves, and other debris atop the carcass. Still, kills attract other lions, as well as coyotes, ravens, vultures, and eagles. In *Soul Among Lions*, biologist Harley Shaw wonders how the kittens keep from becoming meals themselves while their mother is away. They clearly hide some of the time, but they play too, says Shaw. "Kittens seem to have a glorious time at kills," he writes. "Kill sites with kittens present take on a distinctive appearance—that of a minor tornado." The kittens gnaw every bit of bone into small pieces, reports Shaw, and tear up and scatter the hide, ears, and tail of the carcass in a way that suggests they were used as toys.

Mountain lion families drift apart when the young are eighteen months to two years old. The young *leones* gradually hunt farther and farther from their mother, and finally wander on their own in search of a territory. Depending upon the density of their prey, mountain lions require forty to eighty square miles of landscape. Males must find an unoccupied chunk of suitable territory, or challenge a resident male for possession. Young males and oldsters often wander, homeless, poaching food from occupied territories, until they find a niche or die. Females are less territorial; in fact, their domains often overlap. Biologists say that most of the "problem" *leones*, the killers of people, pets, and livestock, are young males between eighteen months and three years old straying beyond the bounds of the usual lion habitat as they search for their own space.

Bans on mountain lion hunting in several western states and booming deer populations have caused *león* populations to swell in the past two decades. At the same time, human populations have grown as well. Cities and towns have mushroomed, expanding into traditional lion territory. The resultant collision has been deadly for lions. In 1995, 120 "nuisance" lions were shot in California, 67 in Oregon, 60 in Montana, and 17 in Utah. If we insist on living in lion country, we must either learn to accept mountain lions' deadly potential—and the risk to our lives and those of our pets and livestock—or we will lock ourselves into a bitter war for space. If we win that war, we will lose *leones*—an outcome that would impoverish us all.

WINTER

Winter is a very different creature across the four deserts. Winter days may bring ice and snow, temperatures warm enough for shirtsleeves and golf games, or days of chill, drizzling rain. Snow is the rule in the northern reaches, including all of the Great Basin Desert, where wintertime lows can drop to forty below zero, and in the higher elevations of the desert's mountains and mesas. In the lowest elevations and most southerly parts of the Sonoran, Mojave, and Chihuahuan Deserts, however, heat still rules in daytime. Storms sometimes dump snow on the higher reaches of these southern deserts, resulting in picture-postcard views of white-capped saguaros and agaves, but even then, snow shovels aren't necessary: the frozen stuff melts as soon as the sun chases the clouds away.

Winter is a wet season for the western deserts, the Great Basin, Mojave, and Sonoran. Unlike the local, violent, and short-lived thunderstorms of the summer rainy season, the winter storms that water these deserts are low-intensity—bringing steady rain or snow for hours or days, dropping smaller total amounts of precipitation, and covering large areas of the region. The Navajos call these gentle storms "female" rain; the blustery summer storms are, they say, "male rain." In the relatively warm climates of the lower elevations of the Mojave and Sonoran deserts, these winter rains wet the legions of annual wildflower seeds, resulting in carpets of colorful blooms.

Winter isn't a wet season all across the deserts. By the time storms from the Pacific Ocean reach the easterly Chihuahuan Desert, they have lost much of their moisture; the precipitation that falls is "mizzle," a misty drizzle, not measurable rain. Winter is usually cool and dry in this desert.

Although winter's lower temperatures make it a quiet time for many desert lives, plants and animals are active year-round in the hot deserts. On warm afternoons in the Chihuahuan, Sonoran, and Mojave Deserts, look for harvester ants out foraging for food, listen for the hoarse calls of ravens, notice jet black pinacate beetles as they walk about, and be alert for rattlesnakes sunning on rocks. Look also for winter migrants that have moved into the deserts from colder climates, including flocks of sky blue mountain bluebirds.

Winter is a wonderful time to explore the hottest parts of the deserts: for instance, visit the palm oases around Palm Springs or the shifting sands of Algodones Dunes in Southern California. Or trek even farther south to see the queer boojum and elephant trees of the Sonoran Desert in Baja California. If the winter has been an unusually wet one, search for annual wildflowers around Anza Borrego State Park in Southern California beginning in late winter. To see snow in unexpected places, visit Big Bend National Park in south Texas. For a fire-and-ice winter contrast, search out hot springs in the snowy expanses of the Great Basin, such as the steaming fountains of Geyser Hot Springs in northwestern Nevada.

CHIHUAHUAN RAVEN

Cuervo llanero
Corvus cryptoleucus

> *I am going to have to start at the other end by telling you this: there are no crows in the desert. What appear to be crows are ravens.*
> —Barry Lopez, DESERT NOTES: REFLECTIONS IN THE EYE OF A RAVEN

NAME: Chihuahuan ravens are named for the desert region where they live. *Cuervo llanero* means "crow of the plains" in Spanish. *Corvus* means "raven" in Latin; *cryptoleucus* means "hidden white" for the white feather bases on their neck that only show when the wind ruffles their plumage.

SIZE: Nineteen to twenty-one inches long

COLOR: Black with purple gloss on back feathers

VOICE: Hoarse croaks and caws

RANGE: Central México north into the southwestern United States from the Gulf of Mexico west to central Arizona; in summer, found as far north as the Great Plains in Colorado

HABITAT: Dry shrublands, grasslands, and deserts

R aven voices wake me on dark winter mornings. Their coughing "chuffs" float in the open window as they flap past, heading for daytime raven business. I swim out of sleep with the delighted realization that it is winter, my favorite season in the desert.

The ravens that I hear are Chihuahuan ravens, also called white-necked ravens for the white patches that show when their black neck feathers are disarranged by the wind. These ravens are unique to the dry Chihuahuan Desert region and the surrounding arid country. Although these black birds look like crows, and their Spanish name, *cuervo*, means "crow," they are not crows. Crows and ravens are both gregarious birds, but crows gather in enormous roosts numbering in the tens or hundreds of thousands of birds. The desert's food sources are simply too sparse to support such dense populations.

Chihuahuan ravens live in the desert year-round, but I notice them more in autumn and winter. As the days become shorter, these slightly-larger-than-crow-sized black birds gather each evening, calling each other out of the sky with hoarse voices, alighting in noisy groups in tall trees or atop utility poles. Often, a single raven will perch on the power pole outside my backyard wall and caw continuously. Its voice acts like a verbal beacon, drawing ravens from all around. First one arrives, circling above the perched bird, and adding its calls to those of the sentry raven. Then another raven flaps in and circles, calling also. Then another, and another, until the cacophony of their calls reaches some critical mass, a level understood only by ravens, and the whole circling mass of black birds flies off together to join that night's roost.

A nighttime raven roost sounds like a city of restless sleepers: the air is alive with mutters, soft cries, whimpers, sighs. The black shapes shift and rustle, jockeying for better positions in the roost trees. Now and then a few ravens will suddenly rise into the air on stiff black wings, then one by one, drift back to settle on the branches again. Ornithologists say that such communal roosting may serve two functions: providing the older, dominant birds with protection from predators and helping youngsters learn to locate food. The less-experienced birds follow their elders as they scavenge each day, gaining expertise in finding food. Back at the roost, the elders take the most protected spots in the center of the flock, leaving the youngsters the most exposed sites at the periphery. For the young ravens, the danger of becoming predator-bait is apparently outweighed by the benefit of eating more often.

Before dawn, the roost splits up, the ravens flapping away in small groups, off to forage for food in nearby deserts, mesquite *bosques*, town dumps, farm fields, or other promising locations. Ravens, like other members of the crow family, are omnivores, eating whatever they find: edible trash, roadkill, small animals, insects, and domestic and wild fruits and grains.

In the golden late afternoon light they gather again, flying toward that night's roost—sometimes in long, orderly lines tracing snakes in the sky, more often in ragged groups, all headed in the same direction as if pulled by a gigantic magnet.

What I love most about ravens is their aerial play: in a group soaring high overhead on flat wings, one will suddenly fold itself like a crumpled black leaf, tumbling earthwards, then pull out and wheel upwards again, cavorting in the air. Chihuahuan ravens sometimes ride the spinning columns of dust devils high into the sky, then coast downwards in playful, dancelike swoops as humans might ride a roller-coaster. In early spring, pairs court exuberantly, soaring together, doing loop-de-loops around each other, tumbling earthwards, then soaring upwards again, one after the other, calling and chasing each other through the air.

Like all ravens, Chihuahuan ravens pair for life but renew their bond by courting each other anew each year. Besides performing aerial acrobatics, pairs perch together and hold intimate conversations in soft raven sounds, fondle each other's bills, and bow and elevate their wings in stylized postures. During courtship, males often fluff out their neck feathers to flash the white bases and pose—much like teenage human males flexing their muscles. Chihuahuan raven pairs return year after year to the same nest site, usually a mesquite tree, or, since trees are scarce in the arid country where they live, a tall yucca plant, a utility pole, or a windmill platform. Nests are often located near where dead animals are likely to be found, at a waterhole, for instance, or a calving pasture on a ranch. Carcasses assure a steady supply of protein—insects and other small animals—to feed growing raven babies.

A raven nest is an untidy, rounded bowl built of sticks and twigs and often held together with bits of baling wire or even barbed wire discarded by humans. Each year the pair refurbishes the nest, the male bringing grasses, bark strips, fur, and feathers, and the female weaving the material into a soft lining. Chihuahuan ravens lay eggs from late April to early June, timing their broods to arrive when warm temperatures and summer rains spawn a relative abundance of insect food.

Driving home one evening, my husband and I spied what looked like a black dust devil swirling a hundred feet or so above the edge of West Mesa. We drove closer, curious. Soon the spiraling mass resolved itself into several hundred Chihuahuan ravens, flapping, looping, and wheeling in a rising thermal like ashes swirling in a hot column of smoke. I have never wanted to fly more than I did at that moment. I imagined what it would be like to take to the air on stiff black raven wings, to launch myself into that upward-rising stream, to spin and tumble and caw and celebrate ravenness. But my body remained firmly rooted to the earth. I reached for Richard's warm hand and together we watched the ravens silently, until finally the swirling column dissolved in the evening sunlight.

Ravens, doing raven business.

CHRISTMAS CHOLLA

Tasajillo
Opuntia leptocaulis

It has been said, and truly, that everything in the desert either stings, stabs, stinks, or sticks. You will find the flora here as venomous, hooked, barbed, thorny, prickly, needled, saw-toothed, hairy, stickered, mean, bitter, sharp, wiry, and fierce as the animals. Something about the desert inclines all living things to harshness and acerbity. The soft evolve out.
—Edward Abbey, THE JOURNEY HOME

NAME: Christmas cholla is named for the profusion of bright red fruits that it carries in winter. *Tasajillo*, "little beef jerky" in Spanish, refers to the look of the stem joints when they are dry. *Opuntia* is from "Opus," a town in Greece; *leptocaulis* means "slender-stemmed."

SIZE: A scrawny shrub up to three feet tall, stems just a half inch in diameter, spines one to 2½ inches long, fruits one to two inches long

COLOR: Stems greenish, grayish, or reddish brown, depending on the season; flowers yellow green to bronze; egg-shaped fruits scarlet

RANGE: From the Sonoran Desert in western Arizona east onto the Great Plains in southern Oklahoma, south into northern México

HABITAT: Often grows within the crown of a mesquite or creosote bush in deserts and grasslands

Winter bleaches the colors from the desert landscape. The green brought by the warm-season rains fades as annual plants die and perennials become dormant. The few plants that retain bright colors stand out vividly. One of these is Christmas cholla, a scrawny cactus that grows in the lower elevations of the Sonoran and Chihuahuan Deserts and is named for the red fruits that dot its stems in winter like holiday decorations.

Cacti are odd plants. Instead of leaves, they sport a variety of spines: fat and curving, thin and wickedly pointed, tiny and barbed. Spines can't produce food by photosynthesis, but they have other advantages more important in the desert: they lose less water to evaporation than leaves, they protect the plant from grazers, and they help shade the stem surface. Cacti stems are unusual as well: they swell after rains as their spongy water storage tissue takes up the vital liquid, and then shrink as the plant uses its stores, emptying each cell. The stems are protected against sunburn —plants sunburn, too—and water loss by a waxy coating sealing their tough skin. Cacti—as well as agaves, yuccas, and some desert grasses—even photosynthesize differently, conserving precious moisture by opening their pores to respire at night rather than during the hottest, driest daylight hours.

Cacti began evolving about 50 million years ago from a group of plants related to roses, after the climate of southwestern North America commenced a series of warm, arid periods, gradually becoming more like today's desert climate. Today, some 1,200 species of cacti grow in the Americas. Cacti come in many shapes and sizes: some are squat and ball-shaped, some are as tall as trees, some grow in dense clusters, some are many-branched like shrubs, some are weak-stemmed, like vines.

Christmas cholla is member of the most widespread and diverse cactus group, the genus *Opuntia*. (A genus is a group of closely related species.) *Opuntias* all possess distinctive stems formed of separate joints, or sections, and unique barbed bristles called *glochids*, that cause great discomfort when they lodge in skin. (Glochids and spines differ: spines are the large needlelike projections that stand out—literally!—from a cactus's stems. Glochids are minute bristles that sprout at the bases of *Opuntia* spine clusters.) *Opuntias* come in two very dissimilar body types: chollas, with cylindrical stem sections and an upright, shrubby growth habit, and prickly pears, with flat, paddlelike stem sections and varying growth habits.

Prickly pear cacti are named for their pear-shaped, edible fruit, a staple food of a variety of desert-dwellers, including wasps, desert tortoises, packrats, cactus wrens, white-winged doves, and humans. To eat the tasty fruit, called *tunas* in Spanish, use tongs to carefully pick fruit that has turned from green to yellow or reddish purple (depending on the species). Brush off the glochids with a bunch of grass or a vegetable brush, wash the *tuna*, then cut it open lengthwise and scoop out the sweet, juicy innards. *Tunas* are delicious fresh or boiled for jelly and candy. The flat pads from *nopal*, the Spanish name for several large species of prickly pear, are edible as well: remove the spines and glochids, cut the pads into strips, and boil them. Eggs scrambled with strips of *nopal*, green chile, and tortilla are delicious, and a traditional dish in some parts of the desert.

Nopales, says Charles Francis Saunders in *Western Wildflowers and Their Stories*, figure prominently in the history of México: it seems that the Aztecs first entered the valley of México as homeless wanderers, not powerful rulers. They roamed, landless and scrabbling for a living, for several generations until one day their leaders saw a sign: a great eagle, with wings stretched to the sun and a snake writhing in its beak, perched on a branching *nopal* cactus. There, on the marshy borders of a great lake, the Aztecs settled and built their capital *Tenochtitlan*—the place of the *tuna*, or prickly pear fruit—now the site of Mexico City.

Cholla cacti may not figure in legend, but they are prominent on the landscape throughout the southern deserts. Unlike prickly pear *tunas*, cholla fruit are small, spiny, and not particularly tasty. But chollas are much in demand for their architecture: supported by a sturdy skeleton of woody tissue, chollas typically grow tall and branch plentifully. Their spiny forms provide protected nest sites for a number of desert-dwelling creatures, including packrats, cactus wrens, curve-billed thrashers, and white-winged doves. Cholla blossoms—like those of most cacti—are simply beautiful. These formidable plants sprout satin-petaled flowers in vivid colors that hark back to their rose ancestors—magenta, purple, chrome yellow, orange, and soft pink.

Christmas cholla is one of the few undistinguished chollas. Its spindly stems are just the diameter of a pencil and not strong enough to support sizable nests. Its thin, needle-sharp spines are scattered haphazardly over the scrawny stems. Even its blossoms are small and unimpressive, the petals greenish or bronze colored. But as fall nights turn cold, Christmas cholla shines when its small fruits blush scarlet, lending an unexpectedly festive air to the winter-drab desert.

COMMON POORWILL

Tapacamino trevil
Phalaenoptilus nuttallii

A fine specimen of poorwill was secured on the evening of July 19 as it was flying over the canyon bottom in front of the house. It would have been impossible to have seen it but for the light color of the ground over which it passed, like a fleeting shadow, in pursuit of insects.

—A. K. Fisher, "A Partial List of the Birds of Keams Canyon, Arizona," THE CONDOR (1903)

NAME: The name *poorwill* comes from this bird's two-note call, a familiar evening sound. *Tapacamino* literally means "flap on the road" in Spanish, a reference to poorwill's habit of roosting on the ground, where its feather pattern hides it completely. *Phalaenoptilus* is "moth-feathered" in Greek, a reference to the soft plumage; *nuttallii* commemorates Thomas Nuttall, a distinguished nineteenth-century naturalist.

SIZE: Seven to 8½ inches long, beak to tail tip

COLOR: Mottled gray brown plumage with white-tipped tail feathers and a whitish collar

VOICE: Males give a low, repetitious, owl-like call that sounds like "poor-will . . . poor-will . . ."

RANGE: Throughout western North America from southern Canada to central México; winters from the southwestern United States southward

HABITAT: Open country, including desert, chaparral, sagebrush, and arid plains

NOTES: Poorwills are related to nighthawks and whippoorwills.

On December 29, 1946, biologist Edmund C. Jaeger and two of his students were hiking in a narrow, rock-walled canyon in the Chuckwalla Mountains of Southern California when they spotted a bird tucked in a shallow niche in the canyon wall, about two and a half feet above the canyon floor. Its plumage blended "so perfectly with the coarse gray granite," says Jaeger in *Desert Wildlife*, "that we had to look twice to convince ourselves that it was really a poorwill." It was, and the bird, pressed into the rock with beak pointed upwards, seemed asleep at first. But when Jaeger touched it, it didn't respond. He picked it up: it was unusually light, and its feet and eyelids felt cold. As he replaced the bird in its rock niche, it slowly opened and closed one eye. It was alive and apparently hibernating, the first bird known to do so.

Common poorwills are insect-catching birds of open, arid country throughout western North America. Their low, repetitive "poor-will" calls are a background sound of spring and summer evenings. These cryptic birds are much more often heard, however, than seen. Roosting on a rock, a low tree limb, or the ground, their mottled plumage camouflages poorwills so effectively that you are likely to step on one before you see it.

Poorwills are crepuscular—active in the cooler hours of dawn and dusk—and they also fly on moonlit nights. (Unlike bats or owls, they are not adapted to hunting in complete darkness.) As the sun sets, a poorwill opens its eyes and becomes alert, watching for flying insects. These narrow-winged birds flycatch from perches or from the ground, darting into the air with beak agape to scoop up food, then returning to perch. Fluttering not far above the ground, a hunting poorwill looks like a huge moth or a silent bat. A special structure inside its eyes improves night vision by reflecting light back to the retina. Bristlelike feathers around its bill function like cat's whiskers, amplifying the sensation of touch to help poorwills zero in on and capture their flying prey, including night-flying moths, chinch bugs, beetles, grasshoppers, and locusts. Agile flyers, poorwills even drink on the wing, fluttering open-mouthed over the water's surface.

The poorwill discovered by Edmund Jaeger and his students returned to its niche in the rock wall each winter for three years. Jaeger and other researchers returned as well to study the hibernating bird. From December through early March, the poorwill "slept" on, apparently unaware of disturbance. The bird was banded and its internal temperature measured every two weeks: its average temperature was 64.4 degrees, 42 degrees below normal poorwill body temperature. Its heartbeat was so slow that it was difficult to detect, and its breathing was negligible. But its metabolism was working, albeit at an extremely low rate—the bird gradually lost weight over the course of each winter.

We now know that other birds go into torpor—lowering their metabolic thermostats to near freezing—during inclement weather or when food is not available. Hummingbirds often drop into torpor overnight to reduce their food needs, white-throated swift nestlings "sleep" thus during periods of inclement weather, and red-tailed hawks slow their metabolisms drastically for short periods when food is scarce. But poorwills can drop their body temperatures lower than any other bird, as low as 45 degrees. These inconspicuous birds, appropriately called *hölchko*, "the sleeping one," by the Hopi, are still the only birds known to regularly spend whole winters—up to three months—in this near-death state.

Poorwills' extraordinary ability to thermoregulate extends to dealing with heat as well. Birds cannot sweat: they pant, mouths open, and flutter the linings of their throat to cool themselves evaporatively from within. Most birds' evaporative cooling is not terribly efficient: they can only dissipate about half of their resting heat production. Poorwills' ratio of evaporative water loss to heat production is the most efficient of any bird; they can dissipate 160 percent of their metabolic heat production by panting and fluttering their throat linings.

Although we know a lot about poorwills' thermoregulation, we don't know much about their family lives. They pair up in spring and nest as far north as southern British Columbia. The female lays two eggs in a scraped spot right on the ground. Since the "nest" offers no protection from the elements or from predators—including Gila monsters, rattlesnakes, and kit foxes—both parents incubate the eggs and feed the nestlings. In bad weather, poorwills may even go into torpor when incubating. The young can fly when they are just over three weeks old, and begin foraging for themselves soon after.

Sitting on the side of Tortugas Mountain one night at dusk, watching the orange streetlights wink on as darkness pooled in the valley below, my husband and I heard a poorwill calling in a nearby arroyo. "Poor-will ... poor-will ... poor-will...." The bird repeated his low call every few seconds, like a chant summoning the night. As I listened, I realized that fifty years had passed since Edmund Jaeger and his students discovered the poorwill wintering in its rocky niche near Joshua Tree National Park. Because of Jaeger's walk in that desert canyon, we now know a lot about poorwills' sophisticated methods of thermoregulation. But we still have many questions to answer before we truly understand the roles these cryptic birds play in desert ecosystems.

COYOTE

Coyote
Canis latrans

    ... *Old Man Coyote is alive and well in the modern world, ... he has survived acculturation (and triumphed over it).*
    —Barre Toelken, Foreword, GIVING BIRTH TO THUNDER, SLEEPING WITH HIS DAUGHTER

NAME: Coyote, in both English and Spanish, comes from the Aztec name for these wild dogs, *coyotl*. *Canis latrans* is Latin for "barking dog," a reference to coyotes' vocalizations. Several American Indian names for the coyote translate as "song dog."

SIZE: Adults forty-one to fifty-two inches long, nose to tail tip, the size of a small German shepherd; desert coyotes weigh twenty to thirty pounds, significantly less than coyotes in more food-rich environments

COLOR: Fur grizzled gray, washed with a yellowish or rusty tinge, buff underparts, tail bushy with a black tip

VOICE: A wide variety of yips, barks, growls, and howls

RANGE: In North America, from eastern Alaska to New England, south through the Midwest and the West into México

HABITAT: Open landscapes, including deserts, shrublands, arid woodlands, agricultural land, and urban areas

Sometimes it is hard to separate coyote, the wild dog, from Coyote, the trickster/hero of American Indian legend. The wily wild canids have adapted so well to life in contemporary western landscapes that they appear in a number of guises: coyote the suburbanite, feeding his young take-out from trash dumpsters; coyote the desert dog, chasing jackrabbits in relays; coyote the rural scavenger, hunting highway verges for fresh roadkill; coyote the city-dweller, trotting down Sunset Boulevard in broad daylight with a smile on his whiskered face.

When Mark Twain traveled from Missouri to Nevada by stagecoach in 1861, coyotes were common scavengers on the Great Plains and the open spaces of the interior West. In his book *Roughing It*, Twain described them as sorry-looking specimens, "But oh, could they run!" When a domestic dog set out to chase a coyote away, says Twain, the wild canid stayed just ahead until the dog was winded, then laughed in the dog's face and pulled away, disappearing in "a whizz and a flash."

Back then, coyotes or "prairie wolves" made their living by following the huge herds of bison and antelope, eating carrion and prey scared up by the larger animals. Soon a flood tide of humans moved into the West, drastically altering coyotes' world: killing the bison, plowing the prairies, building roads, towns, and cities—and slaughtering predators like coyotes by the millions. Many of the deserts' large predators—jaguars, grizzly bears, and wolves—are gone. Others, like mountain lions and bobcats, retreated to protected areas. But coyotes are more abundant now than when Mark Twain wrote *Roughing It.*

How could these wild dogs thrive in the face of such catastrophic changes? Adaptability. Coyotes are masters of flexibility, able to adapt their behaviors—when they hunt, what they eat, the size and composition of social groups, the size of their territories, and even their reproductive timing—to suit the situation. As other large predators were killed off, coyotes took over their niches. The clearing of once-impenetrable forests allowed coyotes to spread from the interior to both coasts. Their adaptability continues to serve these wild dogs well. As urban and city habitat spreads over formerly wild lands, coyotes are moving in next door, their lively voices echoing through town.

Even their enemies admit to coyotes' "devilish intelligence." Such smarts may be linked to their diet: coyotes are omnivorous, gourmands, not gourmets, eating everything from chiles to raspberries to rabbits. Evolutionary biologist John Alcock thinks that coyotes and other omnivores have evolved brains heavy on problem-solving neuron circuitry in order to answer essential questions—Is this food? How can I get it? Over time, omnivores have chosen brains rather than brawn, flexibility and opportunism over stability. Where an opportunity presents itself, coyotes figure out how to grab it.

No wonder that this adaptable, intelligent, flexible animal spawned Coyote, the trickster/hero of so many American Indian tales. As Byrd Baylor writes in *And It Is Still That Way,* "He is Brother Coyote, Trotting Coyote, Changing Coyote, Trickster Coyote. He is everybody's favorite loser. He can be killed but he always comes back to life.... Coyote does terrible things but he does them cleverly. He thinks of things no one else could think of, schemes to trick and cheat and fool his friends—and then he almost always gets fooled himself. They say we learn good lessons from Coyote."

Born in early spring in the darkness of a den dug by their parents, coyotes spend their first month underground with their mother and one to seven siblings, nursing, sleeping, and playing. Their father hunts for the whole family, sometimes helped by a pup from the previous year's litter. Small mammals, like mice, ground squirrels, and desert cottontails make up the bulk of their diet, plus grasshoppers and other insects, roadkill, garden produce, wild fruits, flowers, and berries, pet food left outside, and small pets. Farmers in my valley swear that these wild dogs even raid their green chile fields, eating the succulent and piquant flesh, but spitting out the fiery seeds.

A coyote's hunting "day" begins an hour before sunset, and usually ends an hour after sunrise. Like their other behaviors, however, coyote hunting behavior is flexible. Whether they are cruising the suburbs of El Paso or the wilds of Escalante Canyon, coyotes follow regular hunting routes but adapt their style to suit the habitat. In urban areas, pairs often haunt dining spots including restaurant dumpsters, gardens, parks, and backyards. In wild places, individual coyotes may walk highway verges searching for fresh kills or family groups may team up to chase jackrabbits in relays, one coyote passing the chase off to the next, and so on, until they have run the rabbit into the ground, so to speak. Their appetite for small rodents and rabbits is prodigious: one coyote can eat hundreds of such grazers and seed-eaters in a year, significantly reducing the grazing pressure on desert plants.

By the time they are two months old, the pups spend most of their time outside the den, supervised by an adult. The curiosity that allows them to exploit varying habitats is obvious in their play: they tumble and fight with each other; stalk grasshoppers, adults' tails or anything else that moves; and investigate every sight, sound, and smell in the area. As they grow, they spend less and less time with the family and more time hunting and exploring. In fall, young coyotes leave their family for good and cruise like restless teens, searching for a territory of their own. If vacant niches are not available, however, they may remain with their family—here, too, coyotes are flexible. Depending on the habitat, coyote territories may be as large as 25 square miles or as small as one. Biologists report that young coyotes may wander as far as 400 miles from their natal den—another reason for their rapid spread across the country.

I love coyotes' voices. I often hear them "sing" in the distance at sunset. First one voice begins with high, yipping barks that melt into a full-throated howl. Another joins, threading its own yips and howls into the tune, then a few more choristers add their voices. For several minutes, intertwined coyote voices float together into the night air. Then they dissolve into yips and die away. Biologist Phillip Lehner says that this group yip-howl is a greeting call, as well as a way to declare the area within earshot the territory of a particular hunting group. For me, however, such wild coyote songs bring the desert home.

White Sands Pupfish

Chachorrito
Cyprinodon tularosa

> ... [A]n obscure group of animals that depend on water in an
> improbable place.
> —W. L. Minckley and James E. Deacon, Preface, Battle
> Against Extinction

Name: Pupfishes are named for their seemingly playful, puppylike behavior. *Chachorrito* is the diminutive of the Spanish *chachorro*, or "pup." *Cyprinodon* means "carp-toothed" in Greek, *tularosa* is for the Tularosa Basin, where these fish live.

Size: Adults grow to two inches long and weigh less than a goldfish

Color: Breeding males are iridescent blue above, with a pale blue throat, a yellow orange wash on the fins, and a pale orange belly; females and non-breeding males are olive above and silvery to grayish blue below with vertical barring on their sides

Range: Four isolated springs and streams in the Tularosa Basin, southern New Mexico

Habitat: Clear, saline springs, streams, and marshes with silty or sandy bottoms

Notes: Pupfishes can live five years, although few survive past their third year.

O n a chill, sunny morning, my husband and I joined a tour of White Sands Missile Range, a U.S. Army weapons test facility in southern New Mexico. Unlike most visitors, we were not interested in the sophisticated laser test facilities, the weapons, or the site where the first atomic bomb was exploded. We were looking for fish.

Our small caravan set off up the old state highway that runs the length of the hundred-mile-long missile range, through the desert at the base of the San Andres Mountains. Our destination was Malpaís Spring, a slender thread of a stream that surfaces from the end of a black basalt flow (the *malpaís*, or "bad country," of the spring's name) in the northern part of the range. The shallow, looping channel of the spring runs about a mile from the base of the lava flow before the water sinks into the desert and disappears. This alkaline stream, about a foot across and eight inches deep, is the only water for miles around, yet it supports a unique fish species—in fact, the only fish native to the thousands of square miles of the arid Tularosa Basin, the White Sands pupfish. These *chachorritos* exist in just four springs and streams and were only discovered in the 1950s.

I knelt down and dipped my hand in the slowly flowing water: it was cool, about 50 degrees, and tasted salty. A school of inch-plus-long, chubby fish darted out of a nearby tangle of pondweed and algae: White Sands pupfish. I stood up and looked downstream across the saltgrass flats to a marshy area where the spring outflow vanished into the thirsty desert soil. From where I stood, I could see these pupfishes' entire universe, an improbably narrow ribbon of water running from *malpaís* to desert. How had these fish found this remote habitat? I wondered. And how do they survive here?

Eleven species of pupfish, named for their aggressive, playful, and seemingly puppylike behavior, are endemic to the desert regions of the southwestern United States and northern México. These minnowlike fish were not always desert-dwellers. Until the end of the Pleistocene, some 12,000 years ago, the ancestors of today's *chachorritos* swam in the huge playa lakes that inundated now-dry basins. As the climate warmed up, the shallow lakes evaporated, leaving behind dusty, level-as-dance-floor basins and stranding the tiny fish in the chancy environments of isolated springs, sinkholes, ponds, alkaline streams, and marshes.

As their watery world shrank, the conditions changed drastically: the water grew warmer and saltier, and dissolved oxygen concentrations plummeted. Other fish species died out. Pupfish, however, adapted to these extreme conditions. The different species thrive in water up to five times as salty as the ocean, with temperatures ranging from freezing to a hot 113 degrees. *Chachorritos* can breathe in water with dissolved oxygen concentrations lower than that tolerated by any other gill-breathing fish. Pupfish's ability to shield their renal system from becoming overloaded with salts—the main cause of kidney stones and kidney failure in humans—has attracted the attention of scientists interested in kidney disease.

White Sands pupfish are omnivores—even cannibals—eating the larvae of other aquatic animals, algae, and young pupfish, and they travel in schools. In late spring or early summer, male *chachorritos* put on their breeding colors, turning bright, metallic blue with fins blushed orange. (Females keep their drab colors year-round for camouflage.) Once the water warms to 65 degrees, males stake out small patches of the silty stream bottom and guard them against all competitors, aggressively chasing away male passers-by. If a male has picked a sufficiently attractive piece of aquatic real estate, a gravid female arrives to spawn. She deposits twelve to fifteen eggs in the silt of the stream bottom or on a floating mat of algae; he fertilizes them with a cloud of sperm. The female drifts off; the male remains, defending his territory. Spawning begins in April and continues until September, peaking in July. Each female may spawn repeatedly during the season. The tiny pupfish that hatch weeks later forage for themselves and, if they survive the extremes of their aquatic environment and are not eaten by larger pupfish, spawn the following summer.

These wee fish have adapted to thrive in the specific conditions—water temperature, salinity, and amount of dissolved oxygen—offered by each isolated desert water source. But such precise evolutionary fine-tuning and the rarity of their aquatic homes make *chachorritos* tragically vulnerable to disturbance. Many pupfish species are on the endangered species list, their watery worlds vanishing due to groundwater overpumping and livestock overgrazing, or their lives on the balance because of competition by non-native introduced species. Perhaps the most famous pupfish case is that of the Devil's Hole pupfish, a species living in an isolated sinkhole in southern Nevada. Although their spring, a limestone cavern filled by groundwater, was added to Death Valley—then a national monument—by President Truman in 1952, the water source itself was not protected. After nearby peat mining and groundwater pumping lowered water levels in the cavern and endangered the pupfish, the federal government went to court to secure water rights for Devil's Hole. In 1976, the Supreme Court decided in favor of the fish, declaring that a minimum water level must be maintained to ensure the pupfishes' survival. That decision made these *chachorritos* the smallest organisms to be protected by the U.S. Supreme Court.

At Malpaís Spring, I stood quietly on the saltgrass flat and watched the schools of inch-long pupfish darting through the clear water, pondering the irony that ensures the survival of these particular *chachorritos*. Far off to the south, a missile streaked upwards into the sky. Unlike their many cousins, White Sands pupfish are thriving because they are tucked away inside a sprawling U.S. Army Missile Range. Range officials are proud of the rare fish, says White Sands Missile Range botanist Dave Anderson, and are determined to be good stewards of their habitat. I would never have guessed that high-tech missiles and minuscule desert fish could coexist peacefully. Surely if the U.S. Army can live in a way that allows pupfish to prosper, the rest of us can follow their example.

PINACATE BEETLE

Pinacate
Eloedes obscurus

Long ago, Eloedes was assigned to place the stars in the sky.
Unfortunately the beetle became careless and dropped the stars that then
scattered to form the Milky Way. Being so ashamed for what he had
done, the beetle even today hides his face in the dirt when anyone
approaches.

—Cochiti Pueblo creation story quoted by Floyd Werner
and Carl Olson, INSECTS OF THE SOUTHWEST

NAME: *Pinacate* comes from the Aztec *pinacatl,* for "black beetle"; the English name, pinacate beetle, thus means "black beetle beetle." *Eloedes,* "olivelike" in Greek, refers to the oily black color and the shape of these beetles; *obscurus,* or "covered," is for the hard upper wings that shield their bodies.

SIZE: Beetles grow to 1 ½ inches long; grublike larvae are about an inch long

COLOR: Beetles jet black, grubs whitish

RANGE: Throughout the North American deserts and adjacent arid areas

HABITAT: Open ground from low elevation shrub deserts up to dry woodlands

NOTES: The hundred or so species of pinacate beetles are the most commonly seen insects in the North American deserts.

When I moved to the desert, one of the first insects that I met was a pinacate beetle. Walking to the nearby university campus one warm winter afternoon, I saw a curious black beetle trundling across the sidewalk. It moved with its hind end raised and its head down, as if its rear struts were jacked up too high. I stopped and bent down to watch the beetle. When it noticed me, it stood stiffly and, stretching its long hind legs to their fullest extent, thrust its rear end towards me. That, plus the curious upended walk, gave its identity away: it was a pinacate beetle.

These large, jet-black beetles are so ubiquitous that they have acquired several common names. One, "stinkbug," comes from that comic, rear-end thrusting posture. When threatened, *pinacates* aim glands in the end of their abdomen toward the intruder and spray a black liquid that smells like kerosene and reportedly tastes foul. The noxious spray repels most predators, including ants, scorpions, and tarantulas. Some, however, have learned to disarm the stinky beetles: when a pinacate beetle wanders into a black widow spider's web, the spider simply flings a web line around the beetle to tie it down, and stays out of range until the beetle exhausts its spray. (The *pinacate* must use its pungent defenses sparingly, or risk dehydration: the discharge can account for half of the beetle's daily water loss.) Grasshopper mice grab the beetles and swiftly stuff their abdomens into the soil. With the stinky rear end buried, the mouse can consume the remainder of the juicy beetle at leisure. These jacked-up beetles are also called "tumblebugs," because they look like they are perpetually beginning a somersault. In Navajo, they are called *k'ineedlishii*, the same name given to another common "beetle," the small Volkswagen car!

Unlike many desert insects that pass the cold months in a dormant state, pinacate beetles are active year-round. Their black color acts as a solar collector—in full sun, a black object absorbs 25 percent more solar radiation than a white one—warming these beetles on cool days. Since fewer of their predators are active in winter, the cold months are safer times for pinacate beetles to be out scavenging. Their food, minute particles of wind-blown organic matter, fungus, carcasses of tiny animals, and decaying plants, is just as abundant in winter as the rest of the year. Being black has other advantages: melanin, their black pigment, protects these beetles from ultraviolet radiation and strengthens their shells from being sanded away by abrasive desert soils.

Being black may help these beetles in winter, but it seems as if it would be a liability during the hot months, when getting too warm can be fatal. Pinacate beetles, however, possess a number of strategies to beat the heat. An air space between their wing covers and their back insulates them from the heat absorbed by their black exterior. The air temperature inside the buffer may be 14 degrees cooler than that of pinacate beetles' outer surface. Its ungainly, up-tilted posture keeps this beetle's body high above the hot ground, reducing the heat it absorbs from the soil. One species of pinacate beetle can even exude a waxy substance in times of heat stress, coating itself with an evaporation-resistant layer to help it retain precious moisture. When the heat becomes intolerable, these beetles simply climb into a shady shrub or burrow into the soil. They dig surprisingly quickly, using a side-to-side motion. According to biologist Edmund Jaeger in *Desert Wildlife*, "first all the legs on one side of the body paw at the sand; then these rest and the bank of legs on the other side goes to work."

Some entomologists think that the up-tilted posture and insulating air space of the *pinacate* may help this beetle quench its thirst. As the surface of its wing covers cools at night, moisture in the air could condense on its back. The droplets could then roll down the beetle's slanting body to its head and be channeled into its mouth.

Like butterflies, moths, fireflies, and many other insects, pinacate beetles undergo complete metamorphosis. Their whitish eggs, laid in the soil near a source of decaying plant material, hatch into grub-like larvae, which remain underground, eating voraciously and growing apace, until they have stored enough energy to fuel the transformation into beetles. The two stages of pinacate beetles' life couldn't be more dissimilar: the soft, pale subterranean larvae are essentially immobile and lack protection against heat, desiccation, or predators; the hard-shelled beetles cruise the desert surface swiftly and sturdily, protected by their black pigment and stinky repugnatorial glands. Yet these Dr. Jekyll and Mr. Hyde creatures are two sides of a whole: without the larva and its ability to transform its clumsy body, there would be no beetle. Without the pugnacious beetle and its ability to mate, there would be no larva.

Pinacate beetles may be ubiquitous, but the magical details of their lives save them from being common.

GREATER ROADRUNNER

Correcaminos norteño
Geococcyx californianus

> *Nothing else that lives in the desert, not even a spiny cactus or a resinous creosote bush, seems more at home there.*
> —Joseph Wood Krutch, THE DESERT YEAR

NAME: Roadrunners are named for their habit of speeding across the ground; ours is the larger of two similar species, hence "greater." *Correcaminos* means "runner of the roads" in Spanish, *norteño*, "of the North." *Geococcyx*, or "ground-cuckoo" in Greek, is because this ground-dwelling bird is a member of the cuckoo family; *californianus*, "of California," commemorates where this bird was first described.
SIZE: Adults twenty to twenty-four inches long, beak to tip of tail, wings short and rounded
COLOR: Plumage speckled black and white above, with a greenish iridescent cast, and white below; the bare skin of their legs and surrounding their eyes is bright blue
RANGE: Central California east to western Arkansas and Texas, south into northern México, including Baja California
HABITAT: Open country, including desert, chaparral, sagebrush, mesquite *bosques*, and arid plains
NOTES: Roadrunners are the state bird of New Mexico.

Roadrunners fascinate me—not the cartoon ones, but the real flesh-and-blood birds, two feet long from the tip of their graceless tail to their flashy crest. They strut the dry corners of my yard on long, bare legs, spearing insects and lizards with their strong, sharp beaks. They are year-round residents in the hot southern deserts, thriving despite fierce summer heat, chill winters, wide day-to-night temperature swings, and food armed with spines, venom, and stinging hairs.

During winter, when food is in short supply, other desert residents take to the earth or move away—but not roadrunners. Instead, these carnivores turn to solar energy. First thing each morning, a *correcaminos* hops up on our backyard wall and turns its back to the sun. The bird drops its tail, spreads its wings wide, and lifts the speckled feathers on its back and crest, exposing a "solar panel" of jet black underfeathers and skin. The bird sits there, absorbing heat from the sun, then hops off the wall, and paces away. Ornithologists Robert D. Ohmart and Robert C. Lasiewski found that roadrunners sun themselves to jump-start their metabolisms after dropping their body temperatures overnight to save energy. Many desert birds, including hummingbirds and poorwills, lower their body temperatures overnight. But only roadrunners draw on the sun's energy to warm up, rather than increasing their metabolic rate. By heating their bodies with solar energy, Ohmart and Lasiewski figure, roadrunners reduce their caloric needs by as much as 40 percent—equivalent to humans foregoing the largest of their three meals each day.

Roadrunners also differ from many other desert birds in their choice of locomotion. True to their name, they only fly short hops, hunting on foot, not on the wing. *Correcaminos* are agile and fleet of foot, speeding as fast as fifteen miles per hour across the desert in pursuit of prey: "Watch him race across the sand, full speed, after a lizard. Watch him put out a wing, change his course, throw up his tail, change his course again, plunge headlong into a clump of cactus, and emerge, whacking his limp victim on the ground," writes ornithologist George Miksch Sutton, in *Bent's Life Histories of Birds*. Once a roadrunner stuns or kills its prey by banging it on the ground, the bird, lacking teeth, swallows its meal whole, head first. What doesn't fit hangs out of its mouth (like a child eating spaghetti!), the excess swallowed as the first digests.

Even roadrunners' diet is unusual for a bird. These opportunistic carnivores are renowned for their ability to kill and consume venomous creatures, including tarantulas, centipedes, scorpions, and even small rattlesnakes. It's not that *correcaminos* prefer venomous animals, they simply eat whatever is handy, and many desert animals possess venom. Roadrunners eat a varied diet: large insects such as beetles, grasshoppers, and caterpillars; lizards; snakes; rodents; nestling birds; and birds' eggs. In winter, when meat is harder to come by, they supplement with cactus and other wild fruits, and seeds. Roadrunners compete with coyotes for many of the same foods—a fact which may explain Roadrunner and Wily Coyote's antagonistic relationship in the cartoons.

These fearless and comic speedsters are cousins to cuckoos. Each year, they renew their pair bonds with an elaborate courtship that includes songs, chases, and gifts of food. The males sing to lure in their mates, uttering low, melodic cooing songs, like deep-voiced doves. Pairs chase each other exuberantly through their territory, across the ground, up into bushes and low trees—even across our roof!—down to the ground again, and around and around. The male signals his readiness to mate by bringing his intended an offering. He strides up to her with food in beak, bows his head, and flicks his long tail. If she is agreeable, she turns her back—not a bad sign, in this case—then raises her tail and flicks it rapidly up and down. He hops atop her, the food still gripped firmly in his beak. With much tail-wagging, they copulate. Afterwards, she stretches her beak upwards like a begging chick, mouth open, and he gives her the food. Then he hops off and circles her, strutting, and bowing and cooing.

Like many other desert-dwellers, roadrunners time their mating to the seasonal rains, when food is most abundant. In the Mojave Desert, they nest in spring, after the winter rains; in the Chihuahuan, they court and nest in late summer, after the monsoons. In the Sonoran Desert, if both winter and summer rains are sufficient, *correcaminos* nest twice a year.

Roadrunner pairs share nest-building duties and incubation. They take turns sitting on the eggs during the day, but the male takes the chilly night shift, allowing the female to recoup some of the energy spent laying eggs by dropping her body temperatures 7 to 10 degrees at night. The three to six eggs hatch asynchronously—one to several days apart—revealing featherless, coal black nestlings. If food is short, the parents feed only the older, more aggressive ones. The younger nestlings starve and are eaten by parents or siblings, thus ensuring the survival of at least some of the family and the continuance of their genetic line. Cannibalism is not taboo for most life. It is simply a practical matter, a case of not wasting available calories.

While one parent hunts for food for the hungry nestlings, the other parent stays on the nest, wings spread wide, shading the naked brood from the hot sun. When air temperatures climb above their

101 degree body temperature, roadrunners, like humans, turn to evaporative cooling: they vibrate their throat lining to move air past the moist tissues in their respiratory systems, cooling their bodies from within. Within three weeks after hatching, the young are fully feathered and less vulnerable to the scorching sun. Soon they are speeding across the desert, hunting for themselves.

Correcaminos have personality. One day I watched one sneak away from my neighbor's dog food dish with a beak full of food, crest flat and body hunched like a guilty thief. Another day, a roadrunner raced full-tilt boogie across my yard after a lizard, then paraded with its limp meal onto my patio to swallow it. My dog, who believes that she owns the lizards in the yard, went crazy. The roadrunner simply swallowed its food, flipped its crest up and down, and paced away.

Writing in *The Desert Year*, Joseph Wood Krutch tells the story of a roadrunner that raced him down a rural highway when Krutch was moving to the desert. "It is well, I think, that the roadrunner should greet me at the beginning," says Krutch, "This is his country and there is probably no one who could better teach me about it." Amen.

LICHEN

Liquen
Candelaria submexicana

> *These little guys have not gotten credit over all these years. They're the glue holding this place together.*
> —Jayne Belnap, "Supersoil," SCIENCE NEWS

NAME: Lichen comes from the Greek word for "scab," for these organisms' appearance. *Liquen* is "lichen" in Spanish. (Lichens are so obscure that most have no common name in either English or Spanish.) *Candelaria* comes from the Latin word for "brilliant"; *submexicana* means "below Mexico" in Latin.

SIZE: Each individual is less than an inch across, but colonies may cover much larger areas

COLOR: Orange and bumpy

RANGE: Acidic rocks throughout the southwestern United States and northern México

HABITAT: Rocky areas, from boulders to cliff faces

NOTES: This is one of the most common lichens on volcanic rocks in the Southwest.

I n 1867, Simon Schwendener shocked the world of Victorian science when he announced to the Swiss Naturalists' Club that lichens, then thought to be some sort of "primitive" plant, were actually a sophisticated association between two independent organisms: a fungus and an alga. His theory was pooh-poohed for nearly half a century, until French scientist Octave Treboux successfully grew an algal partner on its own, thus proving that a lichen is actually a composite organism made up of two very different lives.

Lichens are the product of a symbiotic—though not necessarily cooperative and mutualistic—relationship between a fungus, which forms the body, or thallus, of the plant, and an alga or a photosynthesizing bacteria, which provides the food. What you see is actually the fungus; the microscopic cells of green algae or cyanobacteria (once called blue-green algae, but now considered a bacteria) are hidden, woven into the framework of fungus threads. (Different "species" of the composite organism that we call "lichen" are made up of partnerships between dozens of different species of fungus and alga or bacteria. Whether to call the partnership plant or animal is even debatable, since one of the partners—the cyanobacteria—is neither.) Depending on the type of lichen, the thallus can be complex, with up to four separate layers: an upper, protective "skin" formed of fungal threads; a photosynthetic layer of algal or cyanobacterial cells; a storage layer; and then a lower "skin," also formed of threadlike, interwoven fungal stems.

Lichens come in three types. Crustose lichens, like *Candelaria submexicana*, are common on rocks and are often so tightly attached to their substrate that prying them off injures them. Crustose lichens come in neon-bright yellows, acid greens, and fluorescent oranges, as well as less-loud colors. Foliose lichens, named because their flattened bodies sport leaflike lobes, live on tree trunks and on soil surfaces. They are usually green, brown, or gray. Fruticose lichens, like Spanish moss, dangle their filamentous bodies from tree branches and are colored like—and often mistaken for—dry mosses.

One clue to the symbiotic nature of these unusual organisms is their reproduction. Lichens cannot reproduce sexually, since they are comprised of two separate species. To reproduce, the lichen clones itself, forming special thallus buds that contain both fungus and alga or cyanobacteria. However, the individual partners can reproduce sexually *and* separately. The fungus, for instance, produces powdery spores on ascocarps, cups on stalks that stick up above the upper surface of the lichen. If a windblown spore lands in an appropriate environment, it grows into a fungus—it only forms a lichen if it encounters a suitable species of algae. Reproduction of the algal or cyanobacterial partner depends on the particular species.

Lichens inhabit deserts around the world. In order to survive the extremes of desert climates, lichens limit their activity to times when water is available and temperatures are clement, remaining dormant when conditions don't suit. Lacking roots and vascular systems, lichens can only absorb water that actually lands on their thallus surface. Thus, many desert lichens photosynthesize and respire for a few hours in the early morning after "drinking" dew or water vapor from cooler, moister night air, then shut down again later in the day when the lichen thallus dries out. Some desert lichens can revive and grow after being desiccated for over a year and exposed to temperatures above 185 degrees.

When Simon Schwendener announced his lichen discoveries in 1867, he argued that the relationship was a case of piracy: the fungus captured and parasitized the alga. His views were ignored. The collaboration was seen as a classic example of a mutually beneficial relationship. The fungus, it was thought, provided water and protection from the elements, a sheltering structure within which the sensitive alga could survive. The alga, in turn, fed the fungus from its photosynthetic and nitrogen-fixing activities. Then, over a hundred years after Schwendener suggested his piracy theory, botanist Vernon Ahmadjian synthesized lichens in the laboratory and what he saw caused him to think Schwendener was right. When the fungus encounters an appropriate species of algae or cyanobacteria, reports Ahmadjian, its threads actually grow into the microscopic critter's cells, killing many of them. Further, after it is invaded, the alga or cyanobacteria literally hemorrhages food: 90 percent of the edible carbohydrates produced by the photosynthesizing partner's cells moved to the fungus. When the fungus is removed, says Ahmadjian, its former partner recovers and the food hemorrhage ceases.

Whatever their relationship, lichens form a part of what may be the most widely ignored—and most crucial—community in the deserts: cryptobiotic crust, a living layer of mulch that colonizes the upper layers of undisturbed desert soils. Cryptobiotic crusts, says biologist Jayne Belnap, are the ecological anchors of desert ecosystems. These curious microscopic communities check erosion by holding soil particles in place, absorb and retain precious moisture, and fertilize the soils, making essential nutrients available for higher plants.

Cryptobiotic crusts are found in all North American deserts, accounting for up to 70 percent of the living groundcover in desert soils. These vital webs are bound together by filamentous cyanobacteria which grow inside mucilaginous sheaths thinner than the diameter of a human hair. The sticky sheaths wind around individual soil particles as the cyanobacteria grow, literally holding the soil in place so that it cannot be washed or blown away. The sheaths persist—weaving the soil particles together—for decades after their occupants die. Along with cyanobacteria come fungi, which thread their way between soil particles as well; and green algae, which fix nitrogen from the air and thus enrich the soil. Lichens and mosses colonize the soil surface. Dormant during the long months of drought, cryptobiotic crusts (*cryptobiotic* means "hidden life") revive with rain or snowmelt and swell with water, absorbing up to ten times their dry volume. Desert soils that support cryptobiotic crusts show a characteristically spongy surface texture, a result of the gases produced by each living, breathing, digesting community member.

These tough crusts live on for centuries, nurturing and protecting desert soils. They are, however, curiously fragile. Trampling—by human feet, domestic livestock, or the wheels of mountain bikes or vehicles—destroys the slow-growing web. Without the protection of cryptobiotic crusts, desert soils are infinitely less hospitable places: the fine particles wash or blow away, and the remaining soil dries out more quickly and is less fertile. The effect is "dust bowls," says Jayne Belnap. "Oklahoma in the 1930s."

Lichens are small lives, easily overlooked. Yet, whether slowly making soil from the rocks on cliff faces or forming part of the living crust that protects desert soils, they are like the details in a fine painting. Without them, the picture blurs and breaks apart.

NORTHERN GRASSHOPPER MOUSE

Ratón chapulinero
Onychomys leucogaster

> In camp on a still night one often hears a fine, shrill whistle or
> prolonged squeak, insectlike in attenuated quality but as smooth and
> prolonged as the hunting call of the timber wolf. . . .
>
> —Vernon A. Bailey, "Mammals of New Mexico," in NORTH
> AMERICAN FAUNA

NAME: Grasshopper mice are named for their carnivorous diet, which includes grasshoppers. *Ratón chapulinero* means, literally, "mouse that catches locusts." *Onychomys* means "clawed-one" in Greek, referring to the large claws of these mice; *leucogaster* means "white-bellied."
SIZE: Adults up to 7½ inches from nose to tail tip, their thick tail less than a third of their total length; weight, about an ounce
COLOR: Adults gray or cinnamon above, white below; young gray
VOICE: A distinctive, high-pitched, sustained whistle or shriek
RANGE: Below 6,000 feet elevation from southeastern Washington and southern Canada south through the Great Basin and Chihuahuan Deserts
HABITAT: Arid, open country, including grasslands, sagebrush and creosote bush shrublands, and mesquite savanna
NOTES: They are also named "calling mice" for their unusual voices.

The deserts are full of strange tales: lost gold mines, UFO sightings, ghostly mirages. . . . One of the strangest *true* stories, however, has to be the eerie howl of the grasshopper mouse. As mammologist Vernon Bailey described it in 1931, a male grasshopper mouse throws up his head, "and with open mouth and closed eyes send[s] forth its call exactly as . . . a lone wolf give[s] its prolonged howl from the snow-covered crest of a far ridge." The mouse's nocturnal call, a shrill, drawn-out whistle, is a profoundly unsettling noise. Like wolf howls, the call of the grasshopper mouse may broadcast the hunting male's location to his family and declare his territory.

Their uncanny calls are not the only unusual thing about grasshopper mice. While most desert mice eat diets high in vegetable matter, these stout mice are mainly carnivorous, stalking and consuming grasshoppers, pinacate beetles, and other insects, as well as lizards, scorpions, and smaller mice. Skilled hunters, *chapulineros* have developed specialized killing techniques for their varied prey. Grasshopper mice inactivate scorpions' deadly stingers by swiftly grabbing and immobilizing the tail with their front feet before administering the killing bite. They stuff the pinacate beetles' rear end, with its noxious spray glands, into the sand, thus neutralizing its defenses. *Chapulineros* kill their victims the way a mountain lion kills a deer: they break the victim's spinal cord with a swift bite of their sharp teeth just below the victim's cranium.

Holding one of these medium-sized mice in your hand, it is easy to guess their vocation. As mice go, grasshopper mice are husky, built for wrestling prey, not for gracefully climbing into plants to gather seeds. Their tails are short and heavy, hard to grasp in a fight. Their paws are rounded, with elongated front claws for digging and grasping prey, like grizzly bear claws. And *chapulineros'* eyes are large relative to the size of their heads, with plenty of light-gathering ability for nighttime hunting. Their sharp front incisors are no different from other rodent's teeth, but can deliver a killing bite.

Like many desert residents, grasshopper mice live nocturnal lives. During the day, and over the winter, they take to the earth for protection against the extremes of climate, living in extensive burrow systems. *Chapulineros* dig their own homes or remodel those abandoned by other animals, such as ground squirrels, prairie dogs, and pocket gophers.

Grasshopper mice are less common than most desert mice, since their meaty food is less common than the vegetarian fare that other mice consume. Biologists estimate that *chapulinero* population densities average about one mouse per acre, with lower densities where food is less dense. Families maintain hunting territories of around eight acres, large for mice, again because their animal food is so widely distributed.

Chapulineros are rodents and, like all rodents, they are, well— fecund. Biologists estimate that a female grasshopper mouse that begins breeding at two months old can produce fifty-two babies in a year, or as many as eighty-three young in her one-and-a-half year expected lifetime. If each of those mice survived to mate, the desert would soon be overrun with grasshopper mice! Kit foxes, Gila monsters, rattlesnakes, owls, coyotes, and other predators help keep *chapulinero* populations under control. Grasshopper mice mate as early as January in the southerly parts of their range, and continue into the fall. A pregnant female carries her one to seven young for about a month; they are born helpless and with their eyes closed in a special chamber in the family's burrow. The baby mice nurse for three weeks, and then are weaned. Both parents care for the young, which venture off on their own when they are two or three months old.

The three species of grasshopper mice are nearly identical: all are stocky with relatively short, heavy tails, gray or cinnamon upper coats, and white bellies. In fact, they live nearly identical lives, occupying almost the same niche: *chapulineros* hunt the same kind of prey in the same manner, inhabit similar burrows, and raise their young in like ways, but these tiny carnivores occupy separate geographic spaces. The northern grasshopper mouse, as its name suggests, inhabits the northerly end of grasshopper mouse range. The two southern species occupy the southern part of the range, one taking the hotter Mojave and Sonoran Deserts, and the other, the southern Great Plains and the Chihuahuan Desert. Where the northern and southern species overlap, the northern grasshopper mouse lives uphill in the grasslands and piñon-juniper woodlands, the southern species, downhill in the hotter, drier shrub deserts.

When you are out camping in the open desert, listen at night for the shrill, whistling howl of grasshopper mice patrolling the darkness for their prey. Their plaintive call is a reminder of the astonishing diversity of life in the desert.

CREOSOTE BUSH

Hediondilla
Larrea tridenta

　　A breeze stirs the branches and the aroma swirls out of every leaf. I inhale that marvelous scent that graces the air, not cloying, not sweet, but resinous and clean. It's what the world ought·to smell like when it rains.
　　—Ann Haymond Zwinger, THE MYSTERIOUS LANDS

NAME: Creosote bush is named for the pungent tarlike or medicinal odor given off after a rain. *Hediondilla* means "little stinker" in Spanish, also for the fragrance. *Larrea* honors J. A. de Larrea, a Spanish patron of science; *tridenta* means three-tipped, a reference to the shape of the flower's reproductive organs.

SIZE: A shrub three to twelve feet high with an open, airy crown and numerous wiry, blackish stems

COLOR: Flowers bright yellow; seed capsule white and fuzzy, like a miniature cotton ball; small, paired evergreen leaves olive green and shiny

RANGE: Throughout the Mojave, Sonoran, and Chihuahuan Deserts, from southern Nevada and southeastern California east to west Texas and south into México

HABITAT: Well-drained soils of deserts, basins, and mountain slopes up to 5,000 feet elevation

NOTES: *Gobernador,* or "Governor," another Spanish name, recognizes this plant's dominance over an enormous area of the landscape of the southwestern United States and northern México.

L ong ago, darkness just lay there. No earth, moon, or stars had yet been finished," writes botanist Gary Paul Nabhan in *Gathering the Desert,* retelling a creation story of the desert-dwelling Pima and Tohono O'odham Indians. From the darkness came a spirit: Earth Maker, who took from his breast the soil and began to flatten it like a tortilla in the palm of his hand. "From it the first green thing grew: the creosote bush." From the creosote bush, Earth Maker proceeded to create the world.

In the lower elevations of the desert Southwest, it requires no stretch of the imagination to see creosote bush providing the source materials for the making of the world—*hediondilla* dominates these deserts. Its slightly shiny olive green foliage often tints the landscape as far as the eye can see. In fact, creosote bush dots nearly 70,000 square miles of the southwestern United States (an area slightly smaller than the state of Utah), and fully a quarter of northern México.

Although widespread, creosote bush is not widely appreciated. The miles and miles of pure stands of this shrub seem monotonous to many desert-lovers; ranchers consider *hediondilla* worthless, since cattle avoid browsing its resinous branches; some desert-dwellers object to the powerful fragrance produced when its fifty or so volatile compounds are washed off into the air by a desert rain. Regardless, creosote bush is an integral part of the Southwest's deserts, a tough survivor in a harsh land. Its sophisticated strategies to avoid desiccation, sunburn, and consumption by grazers of all sizes may have something to teach us about adapting to life in the desert.

F. V. Colville, a botanist studying the plants of Death Valley, California, in 1893, noticed that the leaves and small twigs of creosote bush are "thinly spread with a covering that closely resembles . . . ordinary shellac." This armor of resins—a complex mix of flavinoids, lignins, volatile oils, saponins, and waxes—makes creosote bush glisten in the sun and impregnates the plant's tissues, inspiring another common name, greasewood. According to Gary Paul Nabhan, desert-dwellers have long collected the beads of amber resin exuded from the plant's stems for an all-purpose patching compound: creosote lac plugs the leaks in boats and engine blocks, waterproofs baskets, and fixes broken pottery.

The resinous armor coating the leaves and twigs acts as a sunscreen, shielding the delicate inner tissues from damage by ultraviolet radiation and excess heat. It also forms a vapor barrier controlling water loss from the leaves, which is critical, since creosote bush, unlike most other desert plants, keeps its leaves year-round, rain or drought. The compounds also repel grazers—from domestic cattle to the tiniest insects—by tasting terrible and forming indigestible masses in most animal's guts. (Remember the last time you ate too many donuts?) Only one small species of grasshopper, a tiny creosote bush cryptic that has no common name and lives out its entire life on the shrub, can digest the protective compounds with the help of microbes in its digestive system. (Botanists call an animal that disguises itself to look like a particular plant a "cryptic.")

Tasting terrible and smelling funny helps *hediondilla* survive in the most difficult desert environments, from parts of Baja California where rainfall is so scanty that four years may pass without significant moisture, to the floor of Death Valley, where temperatures may fluctuate 70 degrees from day to night. Creosote bush's toughness was demonstrated by a thermonuclear explosion at Yucca Flat, Nevada, in 1962, which appeared to have vaporized all of the plants growing at the extremely arid site. But ten years later, ecologist Janice Beatly reported that twenty of the original twenty-one creosote shrubs at ground zero had resprouted and were growing vigorously. Not only does it survive, it thrives. In fact, creosote bush may be the oldest plant known. A creosote bush in the Mojave Desert of Southern California, dubbed "King Clone" for its great age, is estimated to be between 9,000 and 12,000 years old!

Creosote bush may be despised by some, but to others—as the creation story suggests—this scraggly shrub is integral to the desert world. In fact, says Gary Paul Nabhan, creosote bush supplies a virtual drugstore to desert-dwelling Indians: its fragrant branches are used in teas, baths, and poultices to cure a variety of ailments ranging from the common cold to the aches of rheumatism to cancer. Scientists studying creosote bush have confirmed that it functions as an antimicrobial agent—much like penicillin—and an aspirinlike painkiller, and are studying its effects on kidney stones and cancerous growths.

If creosote bush is the fragrance of the southern deserts, big sagebrush, a gray green shrub with twisted stems and felty, three-tipped leaves, is the characteristic odor of the northern deserts, including the Great Basin and the Colorado Plateau. Like creosote bush, the pungent odor of sagebrush is distinctive. And sagebrush is similarly misunderstood. Thousands of acres of the shrub have been killed in hopes of improving forage for cattle—which only eat the peculiar-tasting shrub under duress—or plowed up and replaced by dryland wheat and other crops. Landscapers rarely use sagebrush in their planting plans, even though it is the region's most distinctive shrub. Just like its pungent southern counterpart, sagebrush is often derided as "stinky" and "monotonous."

Sagebrush—again, like creosote bush—is integral to the ecosystems it dominates. A whole suite of animal life depends on this fragrant shrub, including the tiny sagebrush lizard, which eats insects that live in the shrub; the sage sparrow and sage thrasher, both of which nest in sagebrush; the pygmy rabbit, which burrows under and winters on a diet of the shrub; and the turkey-sized sage grouse, which feeds on the foliage and performs its spectacular courtship displays in openings in sagebrush flats. Sagebrush is integral, as well, to some human cultures: the plant's aromatic smoke perfumes American Indian ceremonies throughout the region, including sweat lodges, sun dances, puberty rites, and healing ceremonies.

Smells, say biologists who study human brains, trigger our most vivid memories. My sojourn in the desert began with the distinctive odor of creosote bush. The night my family and I arrived here to live, we rounded the last bend in the highway long after sunset. Darkness hid the landscape, but when we rolled down the car windows, our noses told us where we were. The night air bore a vivid and singular blend of scents—a mix of camphor, citrus, vinyl, tar. I recognized it as the fragrance of creosote bush, the plant Earth Maker used to shape the world. Wherever I go, I'll carry that curious perfume—and with it, my rich memories of life in the desert.

habitat glossary

arroyo A gullied desert watercourse that is dry except after rainstorms or snowmelt, although water may be present beneath the soil surface most of the year. Since they carry additional moisture, arroyos support more verdant vegetation than the surrounding desert and thus more diverse animal life. Arroyo and wash are often used interchangeably. (Pronounced "ah-ROY-oh," from the Spanish word for "gutter.")

bajada The evenly sloping skirt of sediments ringing a desert mountain range. Bajadas form where streams exit the mountains and drop the sediments they carry, forming alluvial fans, fan-shaped deposits with the coarsest material at the top and the finest at the lower edge. Adjacent alluvial fans merge, creating a bajada. (Pronounced "bah-HAH-duh," it means "slope" in Spanish.)

bosque The tangled woodlands lining desert streams and rivers. Bosques are junglelike plant communities dominated by dense growths of deciduous trees such as cottonwoods, willows, sycamores, mesquites, and native walnuts. (Pronounced "BOHS-kay," from the Spanish word for "woods.")

chaparral Brushlands dominated by woody shrubs such as oaks or manzanitas. Chaparral is often a fire-dependent community. (Pronounced "shap-uhr-RAL," from the Spanish word for the protective leggings worn by cowboys when they rode through thick brush.)

ciénaga A desert marsh formed by a spring, a persistent playa lake, or a stream or river. The water in ciénagas ranges from fresh to very saline. Vegetation includes willows, salt cedar, cattails, bulrushes, sedges, and saltgrass. (Pronounced "see-EN-ah-gah," from the Spanish words for "hundred waters.")

desert grassland A desert landscape dominated by grasses. Large areas of desert grassland occur along the uphill margin of deserts, below mountain woodlands. Desert grasslands also occur in swales in basins where fine soil accumulates and water may stand after rains.

mesquite shrublands Areas of desert vegetation dominated by mesquite. These often occur in sandy soils. Where the soil has been denuded, wind-blown dunes may form around the deep-rooted mesquites, burying them almost to their branch tips.

playa A dry, often salty mud flat in a desert basin that drains inward, rather than into a stream or river. Playas are the beds of ephemeral, shallow lakes that hold water only for days or weeks following snowmelt or heavy rains. Although temporary, the waters of playa lakes usually teem with life. (Pronounced "PLY-ah," from the Spanish word for "beach," a reference to the absolute flatness of these landforms.)

shortgrass prairie The grasslands of the western Great Plains, dominated by bunch- or sod-forming grasses one to two feet tall.

shrub desert A desert landscape dominated by shrubs, such as mesquite, saltbush, sagebrush, creosote bush, cactus, or agave, rather than grasses. Shrublands usually occur in areas too hot and dry to support desert grasslands.

swale A hollow or low spot that collects surface water runoff.

thornforest Dry, subtropical woodlands dominated by thorny trees, tall cacti, and shrubs.

wash A desert watercourse that is dry on the surface for much of the year, except after rains or snowmelt. Because the soil stays moist under the surface for longer than the surrounding desert, washes support lusher vegetation and thus more animal life. Often used interchangeably with *arroyo*.

recommended readings
& places to visit

Here are my recommendations for places to read more about these various lives—plus some places to go where you might spot them. These suggestions are just that—suggestions. The readings are my favorites, rather than an exhaustive list of the available literature; nor are my suggestions on how or where to see the plant or creature the only place to visit or the only technique to try.

RECOMMENDED GENERAL READING:

THE AUDUBON SOCIETY NATURE GUIDES: DESERTS, James A. MacMahon, Alfred A. Knopf, 1985.

CADILLAC DESERT, Marc Reisner, Penguin Books, 1986.

GATHERING THE DESERT, Gary Paul Nabhan, Univ. of Arizona Press, 1985.

MOUNTAIN ISLANDS AND DESERT SEAS, Frederick R. Gehlbach, Texas A&M Press, 1981.

THE MYSTERIOUS LANDS, Ann Haymond Zwinger, Univ. of Arizona Press, 1989.

THE SAGEBRUSH OCEAN: A NATURAL HISTORY OF THE GREAT BASIN, Stephen A. Trimble, Univ. of Nevada Press, 1989.

A SIERRA CLUB NATURALIST'S GUIDE: THE DESERTS OF THE SOUTHWEST, Peggy Larson, Sierra Club Books, 1977.

NIGHT-BLOOMING CEREUS: Gary Paul Nabhan's DESERT LEGENDS: RE-STORYING THE SONORAN BORDERLANDS (Henry Holt & Co., 1994), is the source of the epigraph. THE FORGOTTEN POLLINATORS (Island Press, 1996), by Nabhan and Steve Buchmann, describes the relationship between night-blooming cereus and sphinx moths, including a terrifying prognosis for the future of that partnership. For an explanation of sphinx moths' amazing physiologies, read THE HOT BLOODED INSECTS, by Bernd Heinrich (Harvard Univ. Press, 1993). Seeing a night-blooming cereus in flower in the wild is a very difficult proposition, since they only bloom several nights a year and the flowers only last one night. Try Organ Pipe National Monument along the Arizona-Sonora border in July or August.

ROUGH HARVESTER ANT: Bert Hölldobler and E. O. Wilson's book JOURNEY TO THE ANTS (Harvard Univ. Press, 1994) is *the* popular reference on these fascinating creatures, and the source of the epigraph. Susan Hazen-Hammond's article in SMITHSONIAN magazine, "'Horny toads' enjoy a special place in Western hearts" (December 1994), is a good place to start learning about horned lizards. Harvester ant mounds dot the deserts. Look for a low mound, a foot or two across, of tiny pebbles with an ant-sized hole in the middle.

JOSHUA TREE: The epigraph comes from Charles Francis Saunders's WESTERN WILDFLOWERS AND THEIR STORIES (Doubleday, Doran & Co., 1933), an out-of-print book full of charming stories about desert plants. Stephen Trimble's JOSHUA TREE: DESERT REFLECTIONS (Joshua Tree Natural History Association, 1979) is a beautifully photographed and well-written short book about the national park, including information about the yucca trees for which it is named. My favorite place to see Joshua trees in all their astonishing twists and kinks is along the loop road through the northern side of Joshua Tree National Park, between Joshua Tree and Twenty-Nine Palms.

CURVE-BILLED THRASHER: NEW MEXICO BIRDS AND WHERE TO FIND THEM by J. Stokley Ligon (Univ. of New Mexico Press, 1961), the source of the epigraph. The curve-billed thrasher monograph by my father, Robert C. Tweit, in the BIRDS OF NORTH AMERICA series (No. 235, The Academy of Natural Sciences, 1996) is—naturally!—my recommendation for a reference on these understated desert birds. Look for curve-billed thrashers anywhere that mesquite or cholla cactus grow in both the Sonoran and Chihuahuan

Deserts. Look for sage thrashers in summer in the sagebrush-covered basins along U.S. Highway 50 between Ely and Fallon, Nevada.

TUMBLEWEED: The epigraph is one verse from the famous song by the Sons of the Pioneers, Roy Rogers's singing group. James A. Young's article about "Tumbleweed" in SCIENTIFIC AMERICAN (March 1991), is fascinating reading, as is Gary Paul Nabhan's essay "Of Tumbleweeds and Dust," in NORTHERN LIGHTS (Fall 1990). Unfortunately, you can see tumbleweeds all across the North American deserts, especially along roadsides, where they are often the only green plants. Look for monster-sized tumbleweeds in abandoned cotton fields between Tucson and Phoenix, Arizona.

GIANT DESERT CENTIPEDE: The epigraph comes from an old monograph, "Centipedes and Millipedes of Ohio," written by Stephen R. Williams and Robert A. Hefner (THE OHIO STATE UNIV. BULLETIN Vol. 33, No. 7, 1928). INSECTS OF THE SOUTHWEST by Floyd Werner and Carl Olson (Fisher Books, 1994) is a good reference for centipedes and other desert creepy-crawlies. Look for giant desert centipedes at night anywhere in the lower elevations of the three hot deserts. Or visit Sonoran Arthropod Studies, west of Tucson (520-883-3945) and check out their insect zoo.

BURROWING OWL: Hamilton A. Tyler's fascinating book, PUEBLO BIRDS AND MYTHS, (Northland Press, 1991) is the source of the epigraph. For the facts of burrowing owls' lives, read "Burrowing Owl" in the BIRDS OF NORTH AMERICA monograph series (No. 61, The Academy of Natural Sciences, 1993). One of the easiest places to see burrowing owls regularly is the campus of New Mexico State University in Las Cruces. The lampposts in the parking lot east of the campus police station mark their burrows.

RAZORBACK SUCKER: The epigraph is from Wallace Stegner's THE AMERICAN WEST AS LIVING SPACE (Univ. of Michigan Press, 1987), a slender volume that every desert-lover should read. The story of razorback suckers, then and now, is told in "Management Toward the Recovery of Razorback Suckers" in W. L. Minckley and James E. Deacon's BATTLE AGAINST EXTINCTION: NATIVE FISH

Management in the American West (Univ. of Arizona Press, 1991). Razorback suckers still spawn in spring in the shallows of Lake Mojave, a reservoir on the Colorado River between Arizona and Nevada. You have the best chance of seeing these big fish in captivity, at the National Fish Hatcheries in Dexter, New Mexico, and Willow Springs, Arizona.

Saguaro: The epigraph is from Frederick Turner's lucid essay "The Life of Dry Spaces," in his Of Chiles, Cacti, and Fighting Cocks (North Point Press, 1990), a good source of further information on these giant cacti. John Alcock's Sonoran Desert Spring (Univ. of Chicago Press, 1985) and Sonoran Desert Summer (Univ. of Arizona Press, 1990) offer insights into the lives of saguaros and their relationship with other desert creatures. Saguaro National Park, near Tucson, Arizona, is the classic place to see forests of these giant cacti.

Couch's spadefoot toad: Barbara Kingsolver's poignant and hopeful novel The Bean Trees is the source of the epigraph. Read "Frogs and Toads in Deserts" by Lon L. McClanahan, Rodolfo Ruibal, and Vaughan H. Shoemaker in Scientific American (March 1994) for a look at how amphibians cope with arid environments. For a less technical look, try my essay "Spadefoot Toads and Storm Sewers" in Barren, Wild, and Worthless: Living in the Chihuahuan Desert (Univ. of New Mexico Press, 1995). Finding Couch's spadefoot toads means being in the hot deserts after a summer thunderstorm. Listen for these toads' voices at dusk, then follow the sound. Great Basin spadefoot toads emerge on rainy nights in spring.

Ocotillo: The quote comes from a letter in the Douglas T. MacDougal archives at the Arizona State Historical Society in Tucson. Discovering the Desert by William G. McGinnies (Univ. of Arizona Press, 1981) includes a fascinating section on ocotillo. Drive Interstate 10 between Fort Stockton, Texas, and Los Angeles, California, and you can't miss the wiry-stemmed ocotillo "forests" on rocky desert mountainsides. May is the best month to see them blooming.

COSTA'S HUMMINGBIRD: The epigraph comes from a poem by Pattiann Rogers, from her book THE TATTOOED LADY IN THE GARDEN (Wesleyan Univ. Press, 1989). THE BIRDER'S HANDBOOK, by Paul R. Ehrlich, David S. Dobkin, and Darryl Wheye (Simon & Schuster, 1988), is one good source of information on Costa's hummingbirds; Ken Kaufman's LIVES OF NORTH AMERICAN BIRDS (Houghton Mifflin, 1996), is another. My favorite place to watch Costa's hummingbirds is at the hummingbird aviary at the Arizona-Sonora Desert Museum west of Tucson. This museum is a fantastic place to learn about the desert.

BIG SACATON: J. H. Bryne's terse comment on the Chihuahuan Desert grasslands comes from a government document published in 1855, EXPLORATIONS AND SURVEYS TO ASCERTAIN THE MOST PRACTICABLE AND ECONOMICAL RAILROAD ROUTE FROM THE MISSISSIPPI RIVER TO THE PACIFIC OCEAN, Vol. II. Despite the lengthy title, this report makes fascinating reading. THE AUDUBON SOCIETY NATURE GUIDES: GRASSLANDS (Alfred A. Knopf, 1985), by Lauren Brown, includes an informative section on desert grasslands. Papers by many of the foremost experts on the subject are gathered in the excellent book, THE DESERT GRASSLAND, edited by Mitchel P. McClaran and Thomas R. Van Devender (Univ. of Arizona Press, 1995). A wonderful place to see big sacaton as it can grow is at the Audubon Society's Appleton-Whittell Research Ranch Sanctuary, near Elgin in southern Arizona.

GIANT DESERT HAIRY SCORPION: The epigraph comes from Joseph Wood Krutch's classic look at the Sonoran Desert, THE DESERT YEAR (Viking Press, 1963). James Cornett's WILDLIFE OF THE NORTH AMERICAN DESERTS (Nature Trails Press, 1987) is another source of interesting information on scorpions. The best way to find giant desert hairy scorpions (and any other scorpion) is to take a portable ultraviolet light source (a "black light") out into the desert at night. Scorpions' exoskeletons fluoresce in neon-bright colors under UV light.

Screwbean mesquite: Mary Austin's short paean to mesquites comes from THE LAND OF LITTLE RAIN (Penguin, 1988), a classic tribute to the arid country east of the Sierra Nevada in Southern California. For more on mesquites, read GATHERING THE DESERT by Gary Paul Nabhan (Univ. of Arizona Press, 1985). The canyons of Big Bend National Park are a wonderful place to see screwbean mesquite. In fact, the North American grand champion tornillos grow there: the two are nearly the same size, with trunks over three feet around; both are about thirty feet high with crown spreads of forty feet.

Western diamondback rattlesnake: The epigraph comes from Teresa Jordan's beautiful and heartfelt memoir, RIDING THE WHITE HORSE HOME (Vintage, 1994). *The* reference on rattlesnakes is RATTLESNAKES: THEIR HABITS, LIFE HISTORIES, AND INFLUENCE ON MANKIND, by Laurence M. Klauber (two volumes, Univ. of California Press, 1973). Look for western diamondbacks on rural highways at night during the summer (especially after rainstorms). A magical place to search for them is in the flats between dunes at White Sands National Monument in southern New Mexico—especially on moonlit nights, when the pure white dunes glow in the silvery light.

Arizona sister: Robert Michael Pyle's charming and informative HANDBOOK FOR BUTTERFLY WATCHERS (Houghton Mifflin, 1984) is the source of the epigraph. Information on these butterflies' lives is not easy to find. THE AUDUBON SOCIETY FIELD GUIDE TO NORTH AMERICAN BUTTERFLIES (Alfred A. Knopf, 1981), also by Robert Michael Pyle, is a good general reference. My favorite places to see Arizona sisters are in the canyons of southern Arizona's Chiricahua and Huachuca mountains, in summer. Try Chiricahua National Monument in July.

Kit fox: Edmund C. Jaeger's DESERT WILDLIFE (Stanford Univ. Press, 1961) is the source of the quote and a wonderful read on kit foxes. Another good source is SURVIVORS IN THE SHADOWS (Northland Press, 1993), by Gary Turbak. Kit foxes are very difficult to see: your best chance is to camp out in the lower elevations of the hot deserts in spring or summer. Or visit a "living museum" such as Living Desert State Park near Carlsbad, New Mexico or the Arizona-Sonora Desert Museum west of Tucson, Arizona.

TUBE-FORMING TERMITE: The epigraph is from JOURNEY TO THE ANTS (Harvard Univ. Press, 1995), by Bert Hölldobler and Edward O. Wilson. Information on termites is scarce in the popular literature. A good but technical source is "The Natural History and Role of Subterranean Termites in the Northern Chihuahuan Desert" in SPECIAL BIOTIC RELATIONSHIPS IN THE ARID SOUTHWEST (Univ. of New Mexico Press, 1989), edited by Justin O. Schmidt. Look for tube-forming termites' characteristic mud constructions in winter in any of the hot deserts; or turn over cowpies after summer rains to see the tiny white *hormigas* at work.

FAIRY SHRIMP: Stephen Trimble's beautiful and authoritative book on the Great Basin, THE SAGEBRUSH OCEAN, (Univ. of Nevada Press, 1989) is the source of the epigraph. "Miracle of the Potholes," by Rowe Findley in NATIONAL GEOGRAPHIC (October 1975) is a wonderful introduction to these magic creatures. Look for fairy shrimp in playa lakes, shallow, temporary lakes that fill desert basins after spring snowmelt or summer rains, or in rain-filled potholes—natural depressions in the rock that hold water—in the slickrock country of the Colorado Plateau.

SACRED DATURA: Georgia O'Keeffe is the source of the opening quotation, from her book GEORGIA O'KEEFFE (Viking, 1976). Her paintings of datura will show you another way to look at these extraordinary flowers. For more on the uses and dangers of sacred datura, try H. D. Harrington's THE EDIBLE NATIVE PLANTS OF THE ROCKY MOUNTAINS (Univ. of New Mexico Press, 1967). My favorite place to see sacred datura's blossoms is in the red sandstone canyons of the slickrock country of southern Utah.

DESERT TARANTULA: The epigraph comes from Jeremy Schmidt's book, A NATURAL HISTORY GUIDE: GRAND CANYON (Houghton Mifflin, 1993). WILDLIFE OF THE NORTH AMERICAN

DESERTS (Nature Trails Press, 1987) by James Cornett includes much tarantula information. Look for desert tarantulas on warm evenings in late summer and early autumn: walk back roads or trails through the desert and look for palm-sized, hairy spiders.

CALIFORNIA CONDOR: Terry Tempest Williams's eloquent and heart-rending memoir, REFUGE (Pantheon, 1991), is the source of the epigraph. For more information on condors, look up Roger Caras's "biography" of a condor, SOURCE OF THE THUNDER (Bison Books, 1991). Look for the Southwest's newest population of California condors along U.S. Highway 89A, a spectacular drive along the Vermilion Cliffs southwest of Page, Arizona.

FRÉMONT COTTONWOOD: The epigraph comes from THE IMMENSE JOURNEY (Vintage, 1957), Loren Eisley's marvelous meditation on evolution. For more information on cottonwoods, read field guides such as THE AUDUBON SOCIETY NATURE GUIDES: WESTERN FORESTS (Alfred A. Knopf, 1985), by Stephen A. Whitney, or WOODY PLANTS OF THE SOUTHWEST (Sunstone Press, 1989), by Samuel H. Lamb. The largest recorded Frémont cottonwood, nearly one hundred feet tall with a hundred-foot crown spread, grows along the middle Gila River in western New Mexico; another giant grows in the San Pedro National Riparian Conservation Area near Sierra Vista, Arizona.

RIVER OTTER: Gary Turbak's SURVIVORS IN THE SHADOWS (Northland Press, 1993), is the source of the epigraph and a good resource for more information on river otters. The best place to see river otters—sadly—is in captivity at the Arizona-Sonora Desert Museum, west of Tucson, Arizona.

PALLID BAT: The epigraph comes from THE MYSTERIOUS LANDS, by Ann Haymond Zwinger, also a good source of information on bats in general. AMERICA'S NEIGHBORHOOD BATS (Univ. of Texas Press, 1988), by Merlin Tuttle, is a good source for further information. Look for pallid bats hunting in the open desert at night, or join a bat walk given by a museum or park naturalist. For a real bat spectacle, visit Carlsbad Caverns National Park in summer and watch the evening bat flight.

CENTURY PLANT: The epigraph is from Gary Paul Nabhan's GATHERING THE DESERT, a wonderful source of information on century plants. For more on the relationship between bats and plants, look up Donna Howell's article, "Plant-loving bats, bat-loving plants," in NATURAL HISTORY (February 1976). Aldo Leopold's words come from his essay "Conservation" in ROUND RIVER (Oxford Univ. Press, 1993), edited by Luna Leopold. Living Desert State Park, near Carlsbad, New Mexico, hosts a traditional Mescalero Apache *mescal*-roasting ceremony the third week each May.

BIGHORN SHEEP: COUNTING SHEEP: TWENTY WAYS OF SEEING BIGHORN, edited by Gary Paul Nabhan, (Univ. of Arizona Press, 1993) gives an eye-opening range of views of these elusive sheep, from bighorn songs and poems by indigenous desert-dwellers to literary writing to the views of wildlife biologists. The best place to see wild bighorn sheep is at Cabeza Prieta National Wildlife Refuge in the lower Sonoran Desert of southwestern Arizona. Unfortunately, access is limited by the surrounding military bombing range. Another great place to look is in the Inner Canyon of the Grand Canyon.

GILA MONSTER: The epigraph comes from Daniel D. Beck's article, "The Gila Monster in Southwestern New Mexico," in SHARE WITH WILDLIFE, Spring/Summer 1996, a newsletter of the New Mexico Department of Game and Fish. The classic scientific monograph on these fearsome lizards is THE GILA MONSTER AND ITS ALLIES, by Charles M. Bogert and Rafael Martín Del Campo (Bulletin of the American Museum of Natural History, 1956). Look for Gila monsters along desert washes or watercourses on warm summer nights after rains.

MOUNTAIN LION: Ursula K. Le Guin's haunting short story "May's Lion," from her book BUFFALO GALS AND OTHER ANIMAL PRESENCES (Capra Press, 1987), is the source of the epigraph. Reading biologist and lion hunter Harley Shaw's book, SOUL AMONG LIONS (Johnson Books, 1989), will bring you as close as you can get

LIONS (Johnson Books, 1989), will bring you as close as you can get to seeing the world through a mountain lion's eyes. Among my favorite lion haunts: the Chisos Mountains in Big Bend National Park, the ponderosa pine forests of the Mogollon Rim in Arizona, the San Andres Mountains in southern New Mexico, and Zion Canyon on the Colorado Plateau.

CHIHUAHUAN RAVEN: The epigraph is from Barry Lopez's DESERT NOTES: REFLECTIONS IN THE EYE OF A RAVEN (Avon Books, 1990). For more information about Chihuahuan ravens, look them up in Kenn Kaufman's LIVES OF NORTH AMERICAN BIRDS (Houghton Mifflin, 1996) or THE AUDUBON SOCIETY ENCYCLOPEDIA OF NORTH AMERICAN BIRDS (Alfred A. Knopf, 1980), by John K. Terres. My favorite place to look for Chihuahuan ravens is along Interstate 10 between Tucson, Arizona, and El Paso, Texas.

CHRISTMAS CHOLLA: Edward Abbey, perhaps the desert's best-loved curmudgeon, is the source of the epigraph, which comes from THE JOURNEY HOME (E. P. Dutton, 1977). For more on Christmas cholla, look in Lyman Benson's superb THE CACTI OF THE UNITED STATES AND CALIFORNIA (Stanford Univ. Press, 1981). Charles Francis Saunders's WESTERN WILDFLOWERS AND THEIR STORIES is the source of the Aztec story. Winter is the best time to search for these innocuous cacti; look under the canopies of shrubs in creosote bush shrublands.

COMMON POORWILL: The epigraph comes from A. K. Fisher, "A Partial List of the Birds of Keams Canyon, Arizona," THE CONDOR, 1903. For more about common poorwills, read Edmund Jaeger's account in DESERT WILDLIFE (Stanford Univ. Press, 1961). You can hear poorwills throughout the North American deserts in late spring and early summer. Listen for their low calls at dusk near washes or arroyos.

COYOTE: Barry Lopez's book of American Indian coyote tales, GIVING BIRTH TO THUNDER, SLEEPING WITH HIS DAUGHTER (Avon, 1977), is the source of the epigraph and a treasury of cultural coyote lore. Byrd Baylor's charming book of stories told by Indian

1976), also includes coyote tales. For more on coyote the wild animal, read Francois Leydet's THE COYOTE: DEFIANT SONGDOG OF THE WEST (Univ. of Oklahoma Press, 1988), and "The Cost of Coyote Meat: An Update" in John Alcock's SONORAN DESERT SUMMER (Univ. of Arizona Press, 1990). My favorite place to hear coyotes sing is from an overlook on the road to Grandview Point at Canyonlands National Park, Utah.

WHITE SANDS PUPFISH: The epigraph comes from the preface to BATTLE AGAINST EXTINCTION, an eye-opening volume of papers edited by two of the foremost experts on desert fish. FISHES OF NEW MEXICO (Univ. of New Mexico Press, 1990), by James E. Sublette, Michael D. Hatch, and Mary Sublette, has a lucid description of these tiny fish and their lives. Access to White Sands pupfish is limited by the surrounding U.S. Army Missile Range. Visit Devil's Hole, in Ash Meadows Wildlife Refuge in southern Nevada, to see the related Devil's Hole pupfish and to get a sense of how isolated these tiny desert fishes' habitats are.

PINACATE BEETLE: INSECTS OF THE SOUTHWEST by Floyd Werner and Carl Olson (Fisher Books, 1994) is the source of the epigraph and a resource for further information on pinacate beetles. A FIELD GUIDE TO THE BEETLES OF NORTH AMERICA (Houghton Mifflin, 1983), by R. E. White, is another source. Look for these jet-black beetles in winter anywhere in the hot deserts.

GREATER ROADRUNNER: The epigraph comes from Joseph Wood Krutch's THE DESERT YEAR (Viking Press, 1963). John Russell Bartlett's observations come from his two-volume PERSONAL NARRATIVE OF EXPLORATIONS AND INCIDENTS IN TEXAS, NEW MEXICO, ARIZONA, CALIFORNIA, SONORA, AND CHIHUAHUA (D. Appleton & Co., 1856). The description of roadrunner's dashing hunting style comes from Bent's LIFE HISTORIES OF NORTH AMERICAN CUCKOOS, GOATSUCKERS, ROADRUNNERS, HUMMINGBIRDS AND THEIR ALLIES (U.S. National Museum Bulletin, Vol. 1, 1940). Another good source of information on roadrunners is THE BIRDER'S HANDBOOK (Simon & Schuster, 1988), by Paul R. Ehrlich, David S.

Dobkin, and Darryl Wheye. Watch for greater roadrunners sunning on fenceposts in the southern deserts on winter mornings.

LICHEN: The epigraph quotes Jayne Belnap, the world's expert on and leading champion of cryptobiotic crusts, from "Supersoil" in SCIENCE NEWS (December 9, 1989), also a good source of information on cryptobiotic crusts. For the scoop on lichens and their not-exactly-cooperating component organisms, read "The Nature of Lichens" by Vernon Ahmadjian in NATURAL HISTORY (March 1982). My favorite rocks for scoping lichens are the wonderfully sculpted volcanic rocks at Chiricahua National Monument in southern Arizona.

NORTHERN GRASSHOPPER MOUSE: The epigraph is quoted in Edmund Jaeger's DESERT WILDLIFE (Stanford Univ. Press, 1961), which is also a good source for more information on these fierce mice. THE NATURAL HISTORY OF NEW MEXICAN MAMMALS (Univ. of New Mexico Press, 1987), by James S. Findley, is another good source. The only way to hear grasshopper mice is to spend some nights in the open desert. Stay up late around your camp stove and listen for their eerie howls.

CREOSOTE BUSH: Ann Haymond Zwinger's THE MYSTERIOUS LANDS is the source of the epigraph and a marvelous tour of the four North American deserts. Much of my information came from "The Creosote Bush Is Our Drugstore" in Gary Paul Nabhan's GATHERING THE DESERT. My favorite place to smell creosote bush after a desert rain is from my backyard in the Chihuahuan Desert. This shrub is so ubiquitous throughout the hot deserts that you won't have any problem finding it. The same goes for sagebrush in the Great Basin Desert. Try to be in the deserts after a warm rain, and then breathe deeply—and enjoy!